Taking Off the White Gloves

Southern
Women

A series of books developed from the Southern Conference on Women's History sponsored by the Southern Association for Women Historians.

Taking
Off the
White
Gloves

Southern Women and
Women Historians

Edited by
Michele Gillespie
and
Catherine Clinton

COLUMBIA AND LONDON

UNIVERSITY OF MISSOURI PRESS

Library of Congress Cataloging-in-Publication Data

Taking off the white gloves : southern women and women historians /
    edited by Michele Gillespie and Catherine Clinton.
        p.   cm. — (Southern women)
    Includes index.
    ISBN 0-8262-1209-3 (alk. paper)
    1. Women—Southern States—History.   2. Women historians—Southern
States.   I. Gillespie, Michele.   II. Clinton, Catherine, 1952–
III. Series.
HQ1438.S63T34   1998
305.4'0975—dc21   98-27670
                                                                              CIP

Text design: Stephanie Foley
Typesetter: Crane Composition
Printer and Binder: Edwards Brothers, Inc.
Typefaces: Giovanni and Palatino

For acknowledgments, see p. 187

For our second born,
Matthew Colin Pittard
and
Edwin Paul Colbert

Contents

Introduction
1

MARY FREDERICKSON

"Sassing Fate"
Women Workers in the Twentieth-Century South
15

SUZANNE LEBSOCK

Woman Suffrage and White Supremacy
A Virginia Case Study
28

CATHERINE CLINTON

Sex and the Sectional Conflict
43

VIRGINIA VAN DER VEER HAMILTON

Clio's Daughters
Whence and Whither
64

THEDA PERDUE

Columbus Meets Pocahontas in the American South
82

JEAN B. LEE

Experiencing the American Revolution
96

ANNE FIROR SCOTT

Unfinished Business
111

GLENDA ELIZABETH GILMORE

"But She Can't Find Her [V. O.] Key"
Writing Gender and Race into Southern Political History
123

CAROL BLESER

Tokens of Affection
The First Three Women Presidents of the
Southern Historical Association
145

DARLENE CLARK HINE

"A Stronger Soul within a Finer Frame"
Writing a Literary History of Black Women
158

About the Contributors   175
Index   179

Taking Off the White Gloves

Introduction

Putting on white gloves signifies a dozen different meanings, even for southern women. Among women of a certain age throughout the country, white gloves were an indispensable symbol of "ladyhood" and good breeding during their rearing. Young girls were expected to have several pairs to wear for special occasions, and, of course, for Sunday best. As southern women grew older, they learned that white gloves could disguise their calluses, their broken nails, and other telltale signs of women's not-so-genteel activities. More recently, modern southern women don white gloves for prom wear and bridal parties, or pull them out only for Easter. They seem quite an anachronism to most southern women at the turn of the twenty-first century, although white-gloved women are still more a Sunday-morning staple in the South than in any other part of the country.

At the same time, white gloves have considerably different legacies for southern women depending upon their color, class, and heritage. Elbow-length white gloves are a symbol of debutante balls and coming-out parties, whereas short ones can remind us of the days when black maids were required to wear them to serve in white households.

But taking off the white gloves can mean shedding all of these traditions, all of these trappings, to free our hands for meaningful work. Taking off the white gloves means getting down to the "unfinished business" of southern

1

women's history. No longer are we encumbered by these symbols; indeed most of us involved in southern women's history now find ourselves wearing white gloves only when we are handling photographs, prints, or other rare material in the archives. Otherwise we keep the white gloves off, now that we have shed them.

Southern women's historians have been taking off the white gloves for nearly thirty years. In establishing the Southern Association of Women Historians (SAWH) in 1970 at the annual meeting of the Southern Historical Association (SHA) in Louisville, Kentucky, the founders sought to formalize the study of women's history and advance the status of women in the historical profession. (The name of the organization was changed to Southern Association *for* Women Historians in 1983.) Throughout its history, members in the SAWH have worked to end discrimination against women in the profession and to encourage the teaching of and research on women's history, especially that of southern women. Thus, the SAWH has functioned with a dual purpose: to support scholarship on southern women's history and to support all women who are historians in the South.

Over the years the SAWH has constructed a strong professional network that disseminates information about research grants, fellowships, academic positions, and conferences through its newsletters, annual meetings, electronic-mail discussion list, and on-line member directory.

During its first decade, SAWH members firmly committed themselves to fighting sex discrimination, holding workshops at their annual meetings on affirmative action, the Equal Rights Amendment, and sexual harassment, and pressing organizations like the Southern Historical Association and the Organization of American Historians to support committees on the status of women. By the 1980s the SAWH not only had established itself as a leader in the fight for women's equality in the profession but also was a staunch advocate for the burgeoning field of southern women's history.

The Julia Cherry Spruill Publication Prize was first awarded in 1987 to honor the best book published in southern women's history. Julia Cherry Spruill was the author of *Women's Life and Work in the Southern Colonies,* first published in 1938. Thoroughly researched and beautifully written, this work stood virtually alone among books on southern women until women's history began to emerge as a "new" field in the 1960s and 1970s. The Willie Lee Rose Publication Prize was also first awarded in 1987. It honors the best book in southern history authored by a woman. Willie Lee Rose, the author of *Rehearsal for Reconstruction: The Port Royal Experiment* and other significant works, has contributed throughout her professional life to the advancement of women in the profession, and this award seeks to acknowledge those contributions as well as the importance of her scholarship.

The A. Elizabeth Taylor Award was first awarded in 1992 to honor the best article published each year in southern women's history. A. Elizabeth Taylor was widely recognized as "the pioneer historian of woman suffrage in the South." Her essays appeared in the *Journal of Southern History* and state journals throughout the South. The SAWH established this award in honor of Taylor's personal qualities as a leader among women and as an expression of its esteem for one of its founding members.

This advocacy was reflected not only in the endowment of the SAWH's two book prizes and article award, but also through the establishment of the first SAWH conference, devoted to southern women's history, at Converse College in Spartanburg, South Carolina, in 1988. Since this important beginning, the SAWH has sponsored three more conferences at the University of North Carolina at Chapel Hill in 1991, at Rice University in Houston in 1994, and most recently at the College of Charleston in 1997, where more than four hundred participants attended some forty panels. The organization has produced an anthology of selected essays from each of these well-attended conferences that reflects the best and brightest scholarship available in the field.

Membership in the SAWH is another indicator of the organization's stature. From a few dozen committed members in the early 1970s, membership has now climbed to eight hundred, a third of whom are graduate students, a welcome presence that bespeaks a strong future for the SAWH. At the close of the millennium, the SAWH continues to promote women's status, whether as undergraduate or graduate students, junior or senior faculty, archivists or museum staff members, or just plain readers and authors. At the same time the SAWH can boast that many of its members are leading lights at the cutting edge of southern women's history and in southern history as a whole, and it is important to note that the two categories more often than not are no longer mutually exclusive.

The SAWH's success at meeting its original goals is clearly evident at the annual meetings of the organization. Since 1983, beginning with Betty Brandon, the presiding president has had the privilege of inviting a scholar of her choice to give an address to SAWH members and their friends at the annual meeting. These talks have been so well received that it is always standing room only as SAWH members, along with Southern Historical Association members, pour into the hotel ballroom to hear some of the best historians in the business setting the agenda for the writing of southern history.

As editors we have had the great fortune of working with a number of these outstanding scholars. Ten speakers, including one of the editors of this volume, have graciously agreed to let their talks appear in published form in this collection that we have put together in honor of the SAWH on the eve of its thirtieth anniversary.

Collectively, these essays cover a broad time span, grappling with nearly four hundred years of women's experiences in the South, from Native American sexuality and European conquest to black women's protest history in the late twentieth century. Despite the fact that these essays were written at various times across more than a decade, they share a number of important traits, not the least of which is their way of thinking about method. These authors take an "integrative approach," to borrow Virginia Van der Veer Hamilton's term, by relying on multiple combinations of literary analysis, social history, cultural interpretation, labor history, popular culture, and oral history. This layering of methods has produced rich essays peppered with "thick description" that stand as models for innovative, even imaginative, scholarly historical writing.

Despite their varied topics, times, and places, these essays embrace the distinctiveness of the southern past and the distinctiveness of women's experiences within that past. They highlight over and over again the importance of community and place for understanding women's identities, choices, and perceptions. They underline black and white southern women's critical role in the growth of voluntarism in the South, its unique character, and how this voluntarism consistently fostered women's collective action. And whether the essays address southern women in the nineteenth and early twentieth centuries or women historians in the more recent past, they remind us of education's central role in shaping southern women's opportunities and understanding, whether we are examining southern women reformers or women in the historical profession. These pieces also underscore the inextricability of critical categories such as sexuality and gender, race and gender, and women and work for any sort of analysis of southern women's past.

Of equal importance is the insistence by so many of our authors that the personal is political. Their personal as well as their professional experiences have profoundly shaped how and why they have come to understand the past and the present as they do. This recurrent theme highlights the subtle and not-so-subtle ways these authors relate theory to practice.

Southern women, with the gloves off, speak their minds. And the scholars included in this volume are engaged with their subjects and intensely keen on sharing their ideas.

Mary Frederickson, professor of history at Miami University, author of many articles, and coeditor of *In a Generous Spirit: A First-Person Biography of Myra Page* and *Sisterhood and Solidarity: Workers' Education for Women, 1914–1984,* urges us to appreciate the multiple ways women's work has stood as the backbone of southern economy and society. In her overview of black and white women's work between 1910 and 1960 she stresses the peculiarity of women's work in the South in a desperately poor region where women's work was integral to family survival. She emphasizes that race realities have made black women's work and white women's work profoundly different. Further, she demonstrates how women's private coping with poor wages and disintegrating families could be transformed into powerful forms of public resistance.

Suzanne Lebsock, professor of history at the University of Washington, recipient of a MacArthur Award, prize-winning author of *Free Women of Petersburg: Status and Culture in a Southern Town,* and coeditor of *Visible Women: New Essays on American Activism,* enjoins us to see southern women's lives from the inside out, to try to explore from within their worlds, so suffragists and reformers and other women struggling within the confines of early-twentieth-century southern culture can come alive for us. Her careful renderings of the woman suffrage movement in Virginia during the 1910s show how white supremacy was gendered and how opponents to women's suffrage rationalized the debate to undermine the suffrage cause. It was the antisuffragists, Lebsock contends, who argued that universal suffrage meant equal race rights. By linking women's suffrage to the race question, they could condemn advocates of woman suffrage for championing an anti-South and anti–states' rights platform, thereby dooming the southern suffrage cause.

Catherine Clinton, the Douglas Southall Freeman Visiting Professor at the University of Richmond, has produced several books and articles, including *The Plantation Mistress: Woman's World in the Old South, Tara Revisited: Women, War and the Plantation Legend,* and *Civil War Stories.* In her nuanced analysis of mounting sectionalism in the decades before the Civil War, Clinton shows us how both the North and the South "sexualized" each other with their frenzied words and allusions. The language surrounding John Brown's raid on Harpers Ferry becomes a prime example of the power of this gendered sectionalism to wound deeply and alternatively to rally emotional as well as political commitment. For John Brown's raid, like so much of the rhetoric of sectionalism, was viewed by southerners as a powerfully symbolic violation of the South. Once these perceptions were firmly in place, it was an easy task to move from the symbolic to the real when men took up arms against men.

Virginia Van der Veer Hamilton, professor of history and University Scholar Emerita at the University of Alabama at Birmingham, most recently author of *Looking for Clark Gable and Other Twentieth-Century Pursuits: Collected Writings* as well as *Hugo Black: The Alabama Years* and *Lister Hill: Statesman from the South,* has assumed a pioneering role as a woman writing political history. In her essay in this collection, she demonstrates how women historians of the past and even today find themselves "rowing against the intellectual stream." The history of women's entry into the profession is a discouraging one, for women writers of history were long barred from academe's halls or were allowed entrance only as the wives who typed, researched, and often edited their husbands' dissertations and manuscripts. Hamilton points out that even as women have become full members of history departments around the country, they still encounter their share of job discrimination. Because the future belongs to those who shape it, Hamilton contends, women historians must pursue two paths toward equality. First, women must press for more status and power by gaining entrance into departmental and university administrations. And second, women historians must continue to integrate women's history into all aspects of the curriculum.

Theda Perdue is professor of history at the University of Kentucky. Her first book, *Slavery and the Evolution of Cherokee Society*, has been followed by numerous others, all of which have revamped our understanding of Native American societies, including, most recently, *Cherokee Women: Gender and Culture Change, 1700–1835*. In her essay, she took her cue from the conflicted *un*celebrations surrounding the five-hundredth anniversary of Columbus's contact with the Americas. She takes the opportunity to explore an imaginary encounter between Pocahontas and the famous Italian explorer, who sailed under the Spanish flag and was the first to make the dramatic voyage across the Atlantic to claim lands in the Western Hemisphere for European powers. By carefully examining European perspectives on Native American women's sexuality, she shows how Europeans came to justify their conquest and colonization of the New World. Both Spanish and English colonists, despite their allegedly different approaches to colonization, shared in the objectification of sex as well as land. To Europeans, Native American sexuality smacked of wantonness and promiscuity. Indian women's hair plucking, tattooing, and comfort with nudity, as well as their familiarity with sexual jokes and sexual activity, linked them in European minds to the lowest order of prostitutes. Unwilling to acknowledge the whole series of cultural realities that separated European views of sexuality from those of Native Americans, Europeans instead used these differences to condemn, demean, and violate individual Indian women as well as Indian societies as a whole.

Jean Lee, professor of history at the University of Wisconsin and author of the highly praised *The Price of Nationhood: The American Revolution in Charles County*, urges us to use our appreciation for gendered analysis and the approaches it entails to explore the Revolutionary era with far more attention to specificity and place. In this respect, Lee hopes historians will return to careful community studies of the South that help us move beyond our bland generalities and easy assumptions to determine what precisely was exceptional or simply typical about the experiences of everyday people in wartime. What is, she asks us, the deep significance of the Revolution for all those southerners who were allegedly at the periphery of the war, who lived outside the urban seaboard, whose economic lives were linked to Atlantic trade and slave labor? How is this significance shaped by gender, by class, by place? Lee invites us to rethink our approach to scholarship to get at this all-important but too easily overlooked microapproach.

Anne Firor Scott's moving narrative of her own role in southern women's history, and those women who shaped her views, within and outside the profession, provided a fitting talk for our twenty-fifth anniversary. Scott, W. K. Boyd Professor Emerita at Duke University, has published extensively since her first book, *The Southern Lady: From Pedestal to Politics, 1830–1930,* was published in 1972, including her most recent book, *Natural Allies: Women's Associations in American History.* It was Scott's enthusiasm and intensity that sparked the idea for this collection, as she and others suggested we might want to collect our talks—to form a kind of quilt pattern of southern women's history. Perhaps her own *Unheard Voices: The First Historians of Southern Women* made Scott realize how impoverished we are by not having our own sense of ourselves, a missing record of southern women's contributions and accomplishments. Having been elected president of both the Organization of American Historians and the Southern Historical Association, Scott has been given ample opportunity during the past fifteen years to reflect upon her many scholarly and professional achievements. So her confession of those influences that shaped her historical sensibilities and her reminiscences of the profound impact of voluntary associations and women's deep commitment to improving their communities all conspire to provide us with a striking memoir of Scott's career and her ongoing energy for tackling the "unfinished business" that absorbs us all.

Speaking on the twenty-fifth anniversary of the publication of *The Southern Lady,* Scott shows how the writing of women's history has accompanied the history of women's activism throughout American history. She also shows how the growth of women in the profession since the civil rights and feminist movements has changed the very shape of history in a relatively short time. Thus, she predicts that in the future every scholar will have to pay as close attention to the records of women as the records of men. Finally, she urges women's historians to remember that they are collaborators in the writing and telling of history, not rivals.

Glenda Gilmore, assistant professor of history at Yale University, is the author of the prize-winning *Gender and Jim Crow: Women and the Politics of White Supremacy in North Carolina, 1896–1920*. Gilmore's playful title and sardonic tone cannot disguise her serious intent with "But She Can't Find Her [V. O.] Key: Writing Gender and Race into Southern Political History." She shows her commitment from an early age to challenging conventional wisdom as she employs memoir and personal history to unravel the layers of complications facing the new generation of modern southern political historians, herself included. She hammers home a message so many of our invited speakers have emphatically articulated: that gender profoundly shapes both the questions and the answers we explore with our historical research and that its absence may no longer be tolerated. We have diminished racism through raised consciousness and serious commitment to inclusion and changing values during the past quarter century. We must demand equally strenuous efforts to eradicate sexism, which scars and distorts our appreciation of our past.

Gilmore offers detailed accounts of how race and gender prove tightly woven contexts and how this nexus of identity and ideology has powerfully shaped southern culture and experience. Humor, tenacity, and theoretical inventiveness abound within her essay. She demands a new kind of political sensibility and walks us through her own evolution as a compelling case study.

Carol Bleser, Kathryn and Calhoun Lemon Distinguished Professor of History at Clemson University, has published extensively, including *The Hammonds of Redcliffe, Secret and Sacred: The Diaries of John Henry Hammond*, and *Tokens of Affection: The Letters of a Planter's Daughter in the Old South*. Bleser, who gave her address at the SAWH's Fourth Southern Conference on Women's History in Charleston, South Carolina, in June 1997, reminds us that women's writings, often put away and treasured as "tokens of affection," offer invaluable insight not only into the eras in which they wrote, but into their hearts and souls as well. Bleser celebrates the lives and work of the first three women presidents of the Southern Historical Association, who are remembered today principally for their writings. Ella Lonn, Kathryn Trimmer Abby, and Mary Elizabeth Massey dedicated their lives to notable scholarship and professional service for which they received recognition in their later years through their appointments to the SHA presidency. Despite their remarkable achievements, however, these women have been virtually forgotten by the SHA. Time has turned them into mere "tokens of affection." Bleser reminds us not only that we must not forget these women and their important accomplishments but also that we must continue their struggle to improve women's status in the profession by pressing harder for sexual equality in colleges and universities and bringing an end to sexual discrimination and harassment.

Darlene Clark Hine, John A. Hannah Professor of History at Michigan State University, has authored numerous works, including *Black Women in America: An Historical Encyclopedia, Hine Sight: Black Women and the Re-Construction of American History*, and *A Shining Thread of Hope: The History of Black Women in America*. Hine urges nothing less than a revisioning of American history. In her theoretically sophisticated piece, she reminds us that black women's history has been a baptism by fire in which black women have created themselves at the intersections of class, race, and gender. Hine urges us to move beyond traditional conceptions of black women as other to place black women at the center of history and theory and thereby acknowledge and indeed celebrate black women's historical agency across time and place and circumstance. She contends that reading black women's autobiography, in all its many forms, invites new ways of thinking about black women's history and its relationship to women's history, southern history, and African American history and moves scholarship past the first wave that highlighted the exclusion of black women from the historical record to the far more dynamic second wave, where black women are clearly historical subjects. Only when historians refine the frame will black women's voices and their complex pasts be heard and understood. Current scholarship on black women's history, no matter how exciting and rich, Hine suspects, is but the beginning of what will be an incredible outpouring of new scholarship that will transform everything we know about black women and white women and the history of the South and America as a whole.

Although some of these essays are now more than a decade old, they are amazing in their prescience. Each essay identifies fertile ground for younger scholars, inviting new research on a variety of topics. Mary Frederickson reminds us that southern women's work in all its complexity and especially across racial boundaries continues to merit our attention, even as we welcome the pathbreaking work of recent scholars like Jacquelyn Rouse on black women's club work and Stephanie McCurry on women in yeoman households. Suzanne Lebsock's analysis of the suffrage movement in Virginia and its unwillingness to use race and racism as a political tool has its counterpart in new work on suffrage in the Deep South by such scholars as Marjorie Spruill Wheeler and Anastatia Sims. Both Catherine Clinton's and Theda Perdue's engagement in how nations use sex and sexual violence to empower themselves literally and figuratively and to humiliate their enemies is beginning to be echoed in such trailblazing works as Patricia Seed's *Ceremonies of Possession in Europe's Conquest of the New World.* But it is also important to note that more southern historians need to heed Clinton's and Perdue's clarion call. Jean Lee's interest in careful community studies of the Revolutionary era also remains largely neglected, but the thick description she champions is clearly visible in Kathleen Brown's *Good Wives, Nasty Wenches and Anxious Patriarchs* and Gwendolyn Hall's *Africans in Colonial Louisiana.*

What is missing? What should we expect to learn about southern women's history in future annual addresses as we ask a new set of cutting-edge scholars to take off their white gloves? First, we need to remember not to forget the history of women in this profession. Thus, we need addresses that pick up the story where Anne Firor Scott, Virginia Van der Veer Hamilton, and Carol Bleser left off. What is women's current status in the profession? What are we doing to support and promote graduate students? How do we contend with the more subtle forms of discrimination and harassment that affect women in the profession even as we watch the nationwide dismantling of affirmative action?

As we look to the future, we must also look to the past. These representative essays remind us that we must constantly shift our attention to new periods and places. We should anticipate essays that move us beyond the upper South to the multiple Souths of the low country and the up-country, the city and the countryside, the Gulf South and the Southwest. We should expect essays that revitalize the antebellum era, that focus fresh attention on the complexities of the post–World War II South, and that cast us back to the nearly two hundred years that preceded the American Revolution and the early Republic. We should also expect essays that expand our notions about useful analytical categories. For example, we will hear essays that do not pigeonhole "working women" as exclusively twentieth-century industrial workers. We also should expect essays that carefully detail how racial and ethnic differences were constructed in particular places and at particular times in the South and how these constructions shaped gender roles and sexual relations. We can look forward to emerging work on southern culture and lesbian identity. And we can anticipate essays that look at varieties of women's collective action that reach well outside suffrage, labor protest, and civil rights movements. Over the next thirty years, the SAWH will continue to invite scholars to take off their white gloves to document the southern past and all its multiple meanings. We can be grateful for the richness of these offerings as we look forward to the banquet that is to come.

The idea for this book came about several years ago. We contacted those who had given talks since the organization formally adopted a policy of invited speakers. During the past decade, many of these addresses were revised for publication and have appeared in such important journals as *Southern Cultures,* the *Journal of Women's History,* and *Feminist Studies.* We are grateful to be able to reprint these terrific lectures along with several previously unpublished addresses in this historical collection. We know this strong selection of pieces reflects our own history and will add to the growing body of collections that both explains and expands our definitions of southern women's history.

We would like to thank Beverly Jarrett of the University of Missouri Press, whose steadfast devotion to our best interests and continuing support of the Southern Association for Women Historians remains an important mainstay of the SAWH's success.

We would also like to thank the women at southern universities and colleges who helped us to deliver this manuscript. Lisa Phillips and Amy Whitworth of Agnes Scott College and Mary Anne Wilbourne and Deborah Govoruhk of the University of Richmond provided their important support. Most of us in our professional and everyday lives would not be able to do what we do without those women whose invaluable cheer and assistance can prove an immeasurable asset, whose skill and efficiency prop us up and propel us forward on this and several other simultaneous projects.

We also want to recognize that the unpaid labors of dozens of SAWH members have made this book possible, but we especially wish to acknowledge leadership over the past thirty years.

Charlotte Davis / Mollie C. Davis	1970–1973
Constance Ashton Myers	1973–1975
Arnita Jones	1975
Rosemary Carroll	1976
Helena Lewis	1977
Martha Swain	1978
Judith Gentry	1979
Carol Bleser	1980
Elizabeth Jacoway	1981
Jo Ann Carrigan	1982
Betty Brandon	1983
Margaret Ripley Wolfe	1984
Darlene Clark Hine	1985
Theda Perdue	1986
Joanne V. Hawks	1987
Judith Jennings	1988
Virginia Bernhard	1989
Julia Kirk Blackwelder	1990
Marlene Hunt Rickard	1991
Constance B. Schultz	1992
Elsa Barkley Brown	1993
Janet Coryell	1994
Kathleen C. Berkeley	1995
Marjorie Spruill Wheeler	1996
Elizabeth Hayes Turner	1997
Catherine Clinton	1998
Drew Gilpin Faust	1999
Amy Thompson McCandless	2000

SAWH PRESIDENTS 1970–2000

"Sassing Fate"

Women Workers in the Twentieth-Century South

M A R Y F R E D E R I C K S O N

November 1986
Charlotte, North Carolina

There are many paradoxes about women's work in the
South, but none more powerful than the notion that
southern women are pampered and frail, beautiful and
airheaded. The southern lady, the epitome of Victorian
womanhood, has never been permanently relegated to the
arena of cultural myth and image. She keeps reappearing,
sometimes in the flesh (there were apparently a few woo-
ing the judges at the latest Miss America pageant), but
more frequently in a grotesque and inaccurate stereotype
that has masked the reality of women's lives and work in
the southern region.

It is true that this persistent image has obscured the
complexity of middle- and upper-class southern white
women's lives, but it also has had a long-term pernicious
effect on the overwhelming majority of women in the
South. The same economy and society that produced this
regional "lady" has always depended more heavily on
women's labor than that of any other part of the country.
Juxtaposed to the white "lady," and often burdened with
her care and feeding, was the southern black woman who
first toiled in slavery, then near slavery, and who still
struggles to escape the confines of a rigidly segregated oc-
cupational structure that relegates her to the bottom of the
economic scale. Between these two, white lady and black
woman worker, there are other significant groups of

15

southern women, white and black, rural and urban, whose complicated lives are only gradually being understood.

The fate of southern women workers born at the turn of the twentieth century was defined in terms of what was open to women in the 1910s and 1920s. Agricultural labor dominated the lives of southerners, but for most women this meant dependence on husband, brother, or son, for working a farm without male labor was very difficult. World War I increased mobility in the South, and more women moved into industrial work in mills across the region. The incentive of cash wages attracted thousands of women to millwork, but the thrill of earning their own money quickly soured in the speedups of the 1920s and the layoffs of the 1930s. For black women the picture was even more grim. Agricultural and domestic labor defined the options for more than 80 percent of black women from 1900 to 1940.

The southern woman worker contemplating her fate in the early twentieth century was not always pleased with what she saw. She developed strategies to deal with it and to try to shape it more to her liking. Southern workers sassed their fate through personal domestic strategies to cope with the exigencies of daily life and through collective action to improve their work lives. The lot of southern women workers did change, dramatically, between 1910 and 1960, and this was in considerable measure because of the conscious protesting, both public and private, of women themselves.

Because of the economic demand for their labor and the collective nature of their work, white women in industrial jobs began to protest together as early as the turn of the century. The power of their protests became especially visible in the 1920s and 1930s. Because of more severe repression and less economic leverage, black women made less progress in the collective arena until the 1950s. As a result, black women perfected personal strategies to control and influence the course of their lives, and ultimately to change the fundamental nature of their existence in the South.

A powerful force in the working lives of southern women in the first half of this century was the peculiar nature of the southern economy, with its heavy dependence on agricultural and service jobs and its biracial workforce. In 1910, agricultural work and domestic service occupied more than 80 percent of all southern female workers, as compared to 30 percent of their northern counterparts.

Despite the southern industrial revolution of the ensuing thirty years, in 1940 60 percent of southern women workers were still engaged in agricultural and service jobs, with the latter then including institutional service. As late as 1950, fewer than 17 percent of the South's women workers were employed in manufacturing, compared to more than 27 percent in the North.

The biracial nature of the South's workforce is a crucial factor in analyzing the patterns of women's work in the region. Prior to World War II, the majority of women workers in both agriculture and domestic service were black. In 1910, 60 percent of the southern female workforce was black; the figure was 40 percent in 1940. Until the 1960s, although black men held as much as 1 percent of the jobs in some textile mills, and a higher percentage in tobacco factories, black women were stringently excluded from operative positions in textiles and restricted to seasonal handwork in tobacco factories.

This distinctive pattern of women's work in the South has meant that the margin of survival for southern women workers always has been much thinner than for their northern sisters. In 1946 southerners made up 25 percent of the nation's population but received only 8 percent of the national income. Because wage rates were low for all workers, southern families often depended on the wages of two or more family members, and women's wages were more critical to the family economy than in the North. Women working in cotton textiles, for example, typically provided 30 to 40 percent of the family income.

The critical importance of southern women's wages has had profound implications. First, because women's work was crucial to the survival of the family economy, both single and married working women commanded a measure of respect within the family and the community. Second, because of the demand for female labor and the migratory nature of much of men's work in the region, working women, both black and white, could and often did survive without men. Third, through their tie to the outside world of public work women established contacts and networks that supported and often transcended the limited sphere of family and kin. Finally, in an agricultural region like the South, wage-earning women, black and white, were most frequently the ones who led their families off subsistence farms into newly settled mill towns and rapidly expanding urban areas.

Southern working women developed a wide range of strategies to deal with their fate. The majority of these solutions were individual, usually involving other family members. Less common, but more visible, were collective strategies, including plans made with other women, with coworkers or others within the local community. Individual strategies involved marriage and migration, education, controlling childbirth, saving money to buy land, and contributing to the family wage economy. Collective strategies included workers collaborating to help one another in times of need, walkouts and strikes, and various forms of political action.

By piecing together life histories recorded by women in the twenties and thirties, we can document the personal strategies women used to survive and to control their lives. Young southern girls usually became part of a family survival strategy before they were old enough to comprehend the larger picture of domestic economy. On farms, young girls were sent to the fields as soon as they could tell "the beans from the weeds." Often, young black women (and less frequently young white women) earned extra money by cooking or cleaning for families living nearby. Selema Mills of Tryon, North Carolina, resented handing her wages over to her mother, saying, "I got awful tired workin' and havin' my pay took away so regular, so I run off from where I was at and come to town."

Before World War I, as more white families left farms and moved into towns, the pressure to collect wages from children's labor shifted from harvest time to twelve months a year. For some young white women working in the mill was a relief, while for others it was worse than what they had faced before. Rena Austin of North Carolina, who had looked after younger siblings since age three, "loved the mill from the start" because "it was such a change from keepin' house [and] tendin' to babies." Catherine Jones of Huntersville, North Carolina, "enjoyed the mill work more than anything I have ever done." She liked "being with other people and it was so much better than having to work out in the hot sun in the fields." But Elizabeth Callicutt, also of Huntersville, told an interviewer in 1938 that she hated "the mill and everything connected with it." Wages cut down to twenty-five cents an hour, no full-time shifts, and owners and superintendents who took advantage of her made Callicutt discontent, bitter, and determined to leave the mill and Huntersville behind.

Courtship among young southern women, black and white, was the short passage from one family to another and was, whenever possible, rigidly controlled by parents. Cornelia Peterson, a black seamstress born in 1900, married for the first time at age sixteen and remembered vividly the restrictions on her as an adolescent on a Morgan County, Georgia, farm. "We won't allowed to go out, not even to church lessen some of the older folks was with us. And if we had company at home, we had better leave all the doors open in the room where we was at. The old folks didn't turn us free to gallivant round all night, we had to git to bed 'cause we had to work." Charity Doane, a white store clerk in Raleigh, North Carolina, in the late 1930s, grew up on a farm in Wake County, North Carolina. Still single at thirty-two, she criticized her parents for being too restrictive: "If nice boys wanted to call they could come to the house and sit in the parlor and listen to the family sing. We couldn't go out with boys, even in the daytime, unless we had an army with us, and then the boys must be Baptist and Democrats and from a good family."

For many young women, marriage was the easiest and quickest way to leave home. Madame Luck, a black beautician from Georgia, ran away from home and a "mean old stepfather." She remembered being barefoot when she got married and being able to carry everything she owned in "a little 25 pound sugar sack." Mattie J. Wilson of Huntersville, North Carolina, married because she "wanted a home." Marriage usually provided a successful escape, but often not a better life, as Selina Williams of Georgia discovered when she married at seventeen, in 1902. When interviewed in 1938 she recalled: "I had thought many times if I ever did get my freedom I'd do as I pleased, and now that I was married I thought that was my way out. But soon I found out that I had jumped from the frying pan into the fire . . . my young husband was contrary, jealous, and he set out at once trying to boss my every breath and turn. I was just as determined I wouldn't be bossed by him."

Women who did not have to escape from home quickly often could be more particular. Everlina Jane Cotton, a black woman from Cary, North Carolina, "kept telling folks that I wasn't never gonna git married; I didn't for a long time." Finally, she recalled, "I decided that I wanted a railroad man. After about two years, we got married." An interview in 1938 found Alma Kingsland, the unmarried daughter of a white North Carolina farmer, working as a waitress in Raleigh and waiting for "Mr. Right." Kingsland told the interviewer: "I like my men kinda educated and nice, too, and that's what I aim to have." For Kingsland, marriage held the hope of escape, not from home, but from her six-dollar-a-week job.

Once a woman married (if not before), childbearing and its prevention became important considerations. There is demographic evidence that the birthrate among southern women declined dramatically between 1900 and 1940. Women born after 1910 had half as many children as their mothers. There is also qualitative evidence that the use of birth control increased in the 1920s and 1930s as the birthrate declined. During the period between 1900 and 1920, abortion appears (as has so frequently been the case) to have been publicly shunned and privately practiced. After 1920 an increasing number of women in the South, as in other regions, began to openly accept the concept of family planning. Both before and after the watershed of 1920, however, women used abortion as a way of consciously controlling reproduction and deliberately changing the course of their lives.

For example, Ethel House of Raleigh, North Carolina, a white Southern Baptist who took in washing for a living, swore after her second son was born that she "wouldn't have no more younguns." To accomplish this she took "tansy tea, turpentine, quinine, cotton root tea, liniment, kerosene and everything else." Lela Reaves, a white woman living in Negrotown, North Carolina, bore six children after her marriage in 1921 at age fifteen. Determined not to bear another child, she reported that she "lost another one at seven months about four years ago. I done that with a lead pencil," she told the interviewer, "and I near about died." Everlina Cotton had no children, and "ain't never won'ted none." She told the woman who interviewed her, "I don't like chillun—never did. Dey is too much trouble and bother. Dey hold you too tight. . . ."

Everlina Cotton's views about children were probably somewhat unusual. For the majority of southern working women children were an integral part of life, key variables in the family wage economy and insurance against an impoverished old age. But the childbearing years were a time of vulnerability for working women and often a period when the family economy balanced precariously between destitution and survival. For many it was the time when a weak marriage failed or when plans were made to move. For others, the responsibility of children forced women to take control, to buy a piece of land, or to create a job for themselves that provided a measure of self-sufficiency and security.

For example, Elmira Smoot of Hayden, Alabama, a black woman now close to ninety years old, tells with pride of the tactics she used to save $150 and purchase ten acres of land in the 1930s, when her six children were small. Smoot's husband was a sharecropper who worked a different piece of land each year. Known as a "mean man," he "stole everything" his wife earned, and her jobs as a domestic worker supported little more than his gambling. Finally, Elmira grew "tired of running from one place to another" and worked out a plan with her friend and neighbor Laura Watson. The women arranged for Elmira to drop most of her cash wages at a particular spot on the road on her way home. After she was out of sight, Watson would pick up the money and put it in safekeeping. After several years Elmira purchased the land to which she still holds the deed, and the family stopped moving.

The deed to a piece of land provided security in the turbulent Alabama economy of the 1930s, but for women who had already left rural life behind, those who had grown used to depending on their living "coming out of tin cans and paper bags," quests for control took a different form. Of primary concern was access to cash wages, and within that framework women sought as much independence as possible. During the "bad years" of 1930 to 1932 thousands of southern women turned to "odd jobs": sewing, selling flowers, domestic work, nursing, and selling produce. Selina Williams, whose husband ran a small store near Savannah, Georgia, remembered that during those years she "did all my work, helped with the store, kept the children in school, did carpenter work, put up fences, took to sewing to earn money for the family, [and] even half-soled shoes." Crazy-quilt work lives often resulted in women no longer "working out" but, instead, working for themselves. Black women left domestic work to become independent laundresses, seamstresses, cafe owners, and beauticians. White women ran boardinghouses near factories and became seamstresses, florists, and beauticians. Daisy Johnson, a black widow living in Athens, Georgia, opened a beauty shop in 1928, continued to take in washing on the side, bought all her own equipment, and was "mighty proud of the way [her work] progressed." Elizabeth Brittain, a white board-inghouse operator in Georgia, told an interviewer in 1938: "Well, after sixteen years of running a boarding house, I still have plenty of problems to face. . . . But I've been able to make a living and make ends meet, so I guess I've done pretty well."

Southern working women often had to take control of their lives in the face of overwhelming personal abuse and violence. In financially pressed families physical abuse of women and children was commonplace, and young southern girls frequently left home to escape families in which "Papa made us work so hard that we didn't go to school half of the time," or where "Grandpa whipped me so badly . . . that the blood ran out of my body like water." The marriages made by young women on the run often resulted in more abuse, as when Phoebe Simpson of Cary, North Carolina, lost the baby she was carrying after a beating by her husband. "The next time he beat me," she remembered in 1939, years after her divorce, "I was six months gone. He knocked me down and stomped my stomach. I lost that one, too, and I never did git over it."

Although abusive marriages did not always end in divorce, it was common practice for women (and men) to dissolve relationships. Ollie Foster Green, a white Columbus, North Carolina, woman, for example, argued that "husbands was a lot of trouble to me (and Ma), so I made up my mind to do without mine, and make the livin' for myself and the children as long as I could." Mary Wright Hill, a black woman from Asheville, North Carolina, married an "overgrown, spoiled man who wouldn't work." They separated and divorced, and she stayed single fourteen years before marrying again, because, as she put it, "I didn't want any other man having a say so over my children."

Clearly, these women were determined and persistent. They met daily life head-on, uncowed by adverse circumstances and the barriers thrown up by the economic and social realities of southern society. The consistent pattern in their lives is that of fighting back, with a dogged determination to control their fate and ultimately to change it. The individual survival strategies that we have discussed primed women for collective action, and when the opportunity to participate in collective protests arose, lifelong patterns of sassing fate set the stage for women's active participation.

Early in the twentieth century southern women began to organize collectively to protect their wages and to improve their living and working conditions. Their labor activism emerged from the strategies they developed to control their individual lives, both at home and at work. Local, spontaneous, collective actions that established the limits of behavior women were willing to accept from management often expanded into formal labor protests or formed the germ of union-organizing efforts. The grievance of one woman textile worker could, and often did, escalate to involve a roomful of workers, or the workforce of an entire mill or factory. In Henderson in 1927, in Elizabethton, Marion, and Gastonia in 1929, and in Danville in 1930, women were the first to walk out. Female friendship and kin networks, so critical to women's domestic survival, provided crucial support for striking workers, both male and female. Women ran relief stations, traveled throughout the country to raise money for strike funds, and often faced down police and goon squads at the front of the picket lines.

A similar pattern of personal protest spawning collective action emerged for black women's participation in labor activism and civil rights. In the 1910s and 1920s black domestic workers achieved limited successes in local areas across the South; in the 1940s, as black women moved into the southern industrial workforce in greater numbers, they spearheaded organizing efforts in the tobacco industry. After their entry into the southern textile industry, black women took the lead in contacting unions, fighting management's legal obstacles, and establishing interracial coalitions within local plants. From Rosa Parks's refusal to give up her seat on a Montgomery, Alabama, bus in 1955 to the participation of more than one hundred thousand women in the 1963 March on Washington, black women applied personal and collective strategies to the struggle for civil rights.

It is beyond our scope here to explore in detail the extensive role of southern women workers in labor and civil rights protests over the last eighty years. It comes as no surprise that women so skilled at manipulating their domestic situations in order to deal with personal diversity took collective action to resist the institutional forces that constricted their public lives.

This pattern of private coping and public resistance is poignantly exemplified in the life history of a woman who lived, worked, and died several miles from this hotel. Ella May Wiggins, North

Carolina's most enduring folk heroine, embodies the achievement and tragedy of southern women workers' lives in the early part of this century, and crystallizes the history of that period in individual terms.

Wiggins was born in the mountains of Cherokee County, North Carolina, near Bryson City. Her father, James May, was a lumberjack who was killed in a logging accident when Ella was a young girl. Wiggins's mother, Elizabeth, like many southern widows of her generation, dealt with her husband's death by sending her oldest children, Ella and Wesley, to work in a nearby spinning mill to help support the family.

Other strategies, marriage and migration, soon affected Wiggins as well. After a short time in the mill, Ella May married a fellow mill worker named Johnny Wiggins, who, like her father, had worked in the timber region. When word of jobs in the Piedmont reached Bryson City during World War I, Ella and Johnny, accompanied by Wesley, left the mountains to seek work in the burgeoning industrial region of Gaston County, North Carolina. They settled in Bessemer City, where Ella and Johnny took jobs in the American Mill.

Ten years passed during which Ella May Wiggins worked as a spinner, bore seven children, and was deserted by her husband, who left the area without a trace. At age twenty-nine she was a single mother living near her brother's family with a "good man" named Charley Shope, who had fathered her youngest daughter, Charlotte. She sought work on the night shift, in order to stay with her children by day. Money and food were scarce, and two of the children, suffering from malnutrition, developed rickets and died of respiratory infections.

Despite the desperate conditions under which she lived, Wiggins became a central figure in a network of family and friends to whom she looked for support. Her ties to the poor white and black families who lived near her developed into relationships that contradicted the rigid racial mores of the early-twentieth-century South. She understood the plight of southern black workers, for their lives mirrored her own; she came to realize that her future was inextricably bound to the collective destiny of those who lived around her, both black and white.

These stirrings in Ella May Wiggins's mind became more focused

as economic and racial issues in the southern Piedmont gained public attention in the late 1920s. A major strike at the Loray Mill in Gastonia in early April 1929 engendered support from workers in
nearby mills, and Wiggins and fellow employees from the American Mill in Bessemer City soon staged a spontaneous walkout and
joined the National Textile Workers Union, or NTWU. Wiggins
emerged from among the workers in Bessemer City as a strong
leader. Described by one union organizer as "a person of unusual
intelligence," Wiggins frequently led the singing among workers
attending mass meetings at Loray. She seemed to understand each
facet of the complex Gastonia situation and spoke to many groups
of workers about the strike and the union, urging men and women
alike to stand firm in their commitment. Most significantly, Wiggins
sought cooperation between black and white workers. Indepen-
dently, she organized a group of black workers, friends and neighbors who lived near her in Stumptown, a small community outside
of Bessemer City, and brought them into the NTWU.

As events in the Gastonia strike escalated, a mob tore down the
NTWU Gastonia headquarters building and raided the strikers' relief store, the Manville-Jenckes Company evicted more than sixty
families of strikers from company housing, and deputies disrupted
a union rally and broke up a picket line composed of women and
children. A shooting incident in the strikers' tent colony injured one
unionist and four policemen, and fatally wounded the chief of the
Gastonia police. Sixteen union members went on trial, and when a
mistrial was declared an angry mob of more than one hundred men
went on a rampage against the union, wrecking headquarters and
terrorizing, kidnapping, flogging, and threatening to lynch union
members. To protest such lawlessness the NTWU announced a
huge rally of all union people in Gaston County to be held in south
Gastonia on September 14, 1929.

As the events of the Gastonia strike unfolded, Wiggins recorded
them in song. The strike, the union, and the men and women in jail
became the subjects of her ballads. After the murder of the police
chief, Wiggins sang to the strikers: "Come all of you good people,
And listen to what I tell; The story of Chief Aderholt, the man you
all knew well." Drawing from traditional mountain ballads, Wiggins put new words to old tunes while carefully observing the conventions of the familiar songs. These lyrics, "Toiling on life's pilgrim

pathway—Wheresoever you may be, It will help you fellow workers—If you will join the ILD," became a popular strike song. Wiggins, or Ella May as she was always called, sang before large groups
of workers in fervent tones, with great seriousness. As folklorist
Margaret Larkin wrote in 1929, Wiggins's songs were "better than a
hundred speeches." This quiet young woman's untaught alto voice
rang out simple monotonous tunes that captivated those who lis-
tened. Wiggins's six-verse ballad titled "The Mill Mother's Lament"
documented her personal struggle to support her children:

> We leave our homes in the morning,
> We kiss our children good bye,
> While we slave for the bosses,
> Our children scream and cry.
>
> But understand, all workers,
> Our union they do fear,
> Let's stand together, workers,
> And have a union here.

This ballad, as did each of Wiggins's songs, expressed her faith
in the union, the only organized force she had encountered that
promised her a better life.

Ella May was to sing her ballads and speak to the strikers at the
NTWU protest rally on September 14, 1929. Early that morning the
Manville-Jenckes forces mobilized hundreds of men, including
many newly sworn-in deputies and vigilantes, to disperse those attending the rally; they set up roadblocks in all directions. A short
time before the rally was to begin, a group of twenty-two unarmed
union members, strikers, and sympathizers, Ella May among them,
traveled in a truck from Bessemer City to the rally site south of Gastonia. Wiggins had insisted that none of the strikers carry weapons.
The truck was halted at one of the roadblocks, and armed men ordered the workers to return to Bessemer City "on pain of death."
The strikers turned around as ordered, but were pursued by the vigilantes, who attempted to run them off the road. In the minor accident that ensued, most of the workers riding in the back of the truck
tumbled out, and for a moment, Ella May Wiggins stood exposed in
the bright sunlight, leaning against the side rail. Then the mob
opened fire, and Wiggins fell into the truck bed, gasping, "Oh my

God, they've shot me." The other strikers, two of whom were wounded, fled into a nearby field as the mob continued to fire their guns. Wiggins died immediately, in the arms of Charley Shope, who had stood near her in the truck. Seven months' pregnant at the time of her death, Wiggins was survived by five of her children; the eldest was eleven, the baby was thirteen months. They were placed in an orphanage.

The "songstress of the mill workers" was buried in an unmarked grave in Bessemer City's public cemetery. The calm dignity of Wiggins's funeral, attended by hundreds of mill workers, marked the end of the NTWU's organizing efforts in Gastonia. But after Ella May Wiggins's violent death, pressure from local strikers, North Carolina liberals, and national political organizations forced Gaston County mill owners to reduce working hours to fifty-five per week, to improve conditions in the mills, and to extend welfare work in the local villages.

Wiggins sassed fate, and lost, but in so doing she wrested a limited victory for her cause from a powerful and tenacious adversary. In this aspect too, Wiggins's story mirrors the long struggle for autonomy and economic security waged by women workers across the South. The record of the lost strikes and failed unions that dominates southern labor history obscures the fact that women's labor activism has profoundly affected the course of southern industrialization. The outlook for women workers changed dramatically in the turbulent years between 1910 and 1960. The options and opportunities open to the daughters and granddaughters of women born at the turn of the century are vastly different from those of the sixteen-year-old sharecropper's daughter who married in order to leave home, or the fifteen-year-old mill worker who walked through the factory gates for the first time in 1920. Certainly, powerful social, economic, and technological forces contributed to these sweeping changes, but we must not forget the important individual and collective contributions made by women workers themselves. By their tenacious efforts to manipulate their personal lives and collectively improve their work lives, southern women workers did, in fact, alter their fate, transform their lives, and create a better future for their children.

Woman Suffrage and White Supremacy

A Virginia Case Study

S U Z A N N E   L E B S O C K

November 1988
Norfolk, Virginia

When I began the newspaper research for a project on the woman suffrage movement in Virginia, I was reading along in the *Richmond Times-Dispatch* for the summer of 1912. I soon discovered—no surprise here—that the major national story for the summer of 1912 was the sinking of the *Titanic*. The major local story that summer—and here was my first surprise—was a fly-swatting contest. This was part of a public health drive: the *Times-Dispatch* handed out flyswatters to every schoolkid in Richmond and then offered prize money to the children who could slay the most flies. Within days, little Sarah Johnson vaulted into the lead. Sarah's secret was that she invented a fly trap, which put her far out in front of the other children. But then Sarah was challenged by a whole troop of Boy Scouts, who collectively slaughtered enough flies to surge into the lead. But Sarah battled back, and so it went, day after day, Sarah versus the Boy Scouts, on page 1 of the *Richmond Times-Dispatch*.

Last time I told this story in Norfolk, I was still in the middle of the research and did not yet know how the story came out. Today I am delighted to report, for the greater glory of womankind, that little Sarah triumphed, with a total kill of 689,640 flies. Sarah was white; there was a separate contest for black children, and that too was won by a girl, Inez Harris, who killed 236,680. The *Times-Dispatch* concluded that it had been a glorious campaign, a credit to

Richmond, with a total count of 5 million departed flies. This the *Times-Dispatch* believed to be a world record.

As I read along, I kept hoping some alert suffragist would write to the editor, using Sarah Johnson's plucky and inventive spirit as yet more evidence that women should vote. Alas, no such letter appeared, so I have to stretch it a bit to have an excuse to tell about the Great Fly-Swatting Contest of 1912 in a paper that is really about woman suffrage. But it is not such a long stretch. Central to the fly-swatting contest were the battle of the sexes, which the *Times-Dispatch* played for all it was worth, and the separation of the races, which the *Times-Dispatch* instituted as a matter of course. In other words, fly swatting presents one set of possibilities about the dynamics of gender and race; the debates over woman suffrage—which also began in earnest in 1912—present another. And there is the element of surprise in both these stories. Almost everything about the fly-swatting contest was surprising to me. As for the suffrage movement, this project began with a surprise: I was surprised at the relative unimportance of white supremacist arguments in the debates over suffrage in Virginia. At least if we take Aileen Kraditor's work as our starting point, the Virginia case would seem to argue for a reworking of our present wisdom about woman suffrage and white supremacy. Altogether I am working toward trying to understand how white supremacy was gendered, how debate over woman suffrage was "racialized."

I think it is fair to say that the standard interpretation of the southern suffrage movement was set by Aileen Kraditor in her book *The Ideas of the Woman Suffrage Movement,* which was first published in 1965 and is still the standard work on suffrage ideology. The book has one powerful chapter called "The Southern Question"; like the rest of the book this chapter is based on the pronouncements of the movement's national leadership.

Kraditor portrayed the southern suffragists chiefly as agents of white supremacy; the "principal argument" of the southern suffragists, according to Kraditor, was that granting votes to women would enhance white political dominion in the South. (The basic reasoning here was that since there were more white women in the South than there were black men and black women put together, woman suffrage would make white supremacy more secure than ever.) Two further points about Kraditor, and then I will get to the Virginia case: First, according to Kraditor, suffragists and antisuffragists were all pretty much alike when it came to dealing with voters they regarded as undesirables—both blacks and the foreign born. Both suffragists and antis agreed that blacks and certain immigrant groups were unfit to vote; the only point of difference between them was on how to prevent those groups from attaining real power, with suffragists of course arguing that votes for women would mean that more of the "right" people would be voting, while antis predicted that more of the "wrong" people would be voting. The differences between the suffragists and their opponents, then, were merely tactical.

Second, Kraditor's central interest was in how movements change over time, and the context for her observations about white supremacy was the early women's rights movement. Given the abolitionist commitments of the early women's rights leaders, the appearance of white supremacist thinking is indeed significant. And this is one more plank in Kraditor's larger argument, which is to demonstrate how the movement resorted to "expediency," and how it made itself respectable in order to win.

Now to some extent Kraditor's argument will stand for the ages. *Of course* the suffrage movement made itself more respectable; you do not get the Constitution of the United States amended by calling yourself a bolshevik. But I want to shift the context, to look at woman suffrage and white supremacy not at the level of national ideology but in the context where it was fought out state by state, the context of close-to-the-ground local politics. I also want to expand the cast of characters so that we add two groups, African Americans and the antisuffragists. The results, so far, are two. First, I am going to do a partial rehabilitation of the reputation of the white woman suffragists, something they have coming. That is the easy part. And second, I want to grope toward some analytic frameworks that might help us understand the southern suffrage movement more fully.

First, the political context. The woman suffrage movement in Virginia was organized in 1909; the antis organized three years later, when woman suffrage came before the general assembly for the first time. The story of Virginia politics in the decade that preceded the organization of the suffrage forces in Virginia was of a resolute, relentless, successful movement to destroy black political participation. The centerpiece was the constitution of 1902, written with the express purpose of disfranchising black men. A great many lower-class whites were also disfranchised. The 1902 constitution in fact threatened to disfranchise so many whites that the framers did not dare submit it to the voters for ratification. They simply promulgated it as the new supreme law of the Commonwealth.

The Virginia electorate, in one stroke, was cut in half. The Republican Party was nearly destroyed, and the stage was set for the triumph of a Democratic machine dedicated to minimal government and keeping itself in power. But even though the machine (or "the Organization") did succeed in winning control of the state, it is important to realize that this was not the finale; the white men who ran the state felt they could never do enough to secure white supremacy, and during the ten years plus in which woman suffrage was at issue in Virginia those men did one low-down thing after another. Race baiting remained an effective tactic in political campaigns. The Democrats saw to it that no blacks could vote in their primaries. The Republicans, who had traditionally included substantial numbers of black men in their ranks, tried to purge their remaining black members, hoping in that way to attract white defectors from the Democrats. This was bigotry that did not quit. It is also important to recognize that this was the age of legally mandated segregation; as in most other southern states, the Virginia legislature took steps to segregate everything that was not segregated already. Local ordinances did likewise.

Given that context, the wonder is that the woman suffrage campaign kicked up so little in the way of racial arguments. I read all of the *Richmond Times-Dispatch* from 1912, when woman suffrage was brought to the legislature for the first time, to 1920, when the legislature defeated woman suffrage for the last time. A rough count for that period results in the following numbers: There were more than four hundred letters to the editor about suffrage, both pro and con, and 8 percent of them made explicit mention of the race question. There were also more than two hundred editorials on woman suffrage; only 4 percent of them explicitly mentioned the alleged menace of the black voter.

Other hunting grounds yielded even less in the way of racial arguments. The *Times-Dispatch* reported on all the conventions of the Equal Suffrage League of Virginia and printed dozens of routine summaries of speeches delivered at meetings of the Richmond Suffrage League. If anyone breathed a word about white supremacy, it was not reported here. There was nothing about the black vote in the suffragists' own short-lived newspaper or in the suffrage edition of the *Richmond News-Leader* published in 1914. Finally, in the archives of the Norfolk Equal Suffrage League there is a paper listing "Stock arguments we had to meet over and over." None of them were racial arguments.

Again, in view of Kraditor's thesis, this is a surprise. The great bulk of woman suffrage propaganda, both pro and anti, conveyed the same arguments that predominated in the rest of the country. They argued about whether the vote was a privilege or a natural right. They went back and forth about whether the vote would make women better mothers and what the vote would do to the home, or for the home. They wrangled over how the ballot might affect women's roles in the reform movements of the day, and in that connection they offered differing interpretations of the reform legislation that had been enacted in states where women already had the vote. They debated whether women really wanted to vote, and whether it mattered whether women wanted it. They fought over the question of whether woman suffrage was inevitable. They resorted to guilt by association—though I must say the antis were more culpable than the suffragists here—with the antis accusing the suffragists of being cozy with socialists, anarchists, and (after the Russian Revolution) bolsheviks. So, all in all, the arguments came straight from the national book.

There were a couple of arguments with more local resonance. One was states' rights, a very serious issue that I will get to in time. The other was the question of whether Thomas Jefferson would be a suffragist if he were still alive. This was not a meaningless question, given the fact that a legislator, speaking before his colleagues, could still count on ritual applause whenever he invoked the name of Jefferson or Patrick Henry or Robert E. Lee. (The suffragists sometimes tried to buttress their own authority on such questions by emphasizing their literal descent from Founding Fathers. Lucy Randolph Mason had a particularly illustrious ancestry that included George Mason and John Marshall. Adele Clark, a suffragist who lived to be more than one hundred, was interviewed in the 1970s and was still reciting Lucy Randolph Mason's pedigree.)

And there was, eventually, a white supremacist argument. The antis started it, and they elaborated it in increasingly scurrilous ways as the suffrage forces won more victories nationwide. When I say "antis" I am referring to a congeries of Virginians, including the Virginia Association Opposed to Woman Suffrage (an organization of socially prominent white women and their husbands), along with various public officials, newspaper editors, and others who went on public record as opposing votes for women. All of these people, except one, were white. The one black anti whom I have found was a story in herself. Her name was Nannie Goode, and she became momentarily famous when she won an essay contest sponsored by one of the Richmond newspapers. The contest was for the best antisuffrage essay; Nannie Goode's essay was judged by a blind jury to be the best, her essay was printed in the paper, and the editor appended a note asking her to send in her picture as well. Mrs. Goode did so. The editor was nonplussed to say the least, never ran the picture, and never mentioned the essay contest again. The national black press got hold of it, though, and had a wonderful time.

When I say suffragists, I am in most cases referring to the active leadership of the Equal Suffrage League. Like the antis, these also tended to be socially prominent white women—Masons and Randolphs—who had some male allies: some clergymen, a few public officials, a very occasional editor, some labor leaders. There were black suffragists, too, but for reasons I will explore shortly, they were very, very quiet.

The legislature considered woman suffrage amendments to the state constitution in 1912 and again in 1914. In both sessions the suffrage amendment was trounced (twelve to eighty-five, thirteen to seventy-four). In the course of those and other debates, antisuffragists did make some racist attacks on woman suffrage, but these were sporadic, and the suffragists chose to ignore them. The argument became focused in 1915 when a Richmond editor published an editorial claiming that there were twenty-nine counties in Virginia with black majorities, and that every one of those counties would be "condemned" to black rule if women were granted the vote. The antis clearly thought they had something here: the editorial was reprinted in broadside form, and it found its way into newspapers all over the state.

This time the suffragists felt they had to respond, and having

decided to respond did so in their usual way. They did their home-
work, they consulted lawyers, and they wrote measured, educated
rebuttals. In the process they formulated the argument that would
serve them for the remainder of the suffrage campaign. In one
sentence, their argument was that white supremacy was not at
issue. First, they pointed out that white women outnumbered black
women in two-thirds of Virginia's counties. Second, they denied
that counties with black majorities were in any danger of black rule;
the constitutional restrictions already in place would continue to
serve the purposes for which they were enacted. There was a poll
tax. There was a literacy test (the suffragists explained that the illiteracy rate among blacks was significantly higher than that among
whites—22 percent compared to 8 percent). And there was one pro-
vision in the constitution that had not even been used yet: any
county in which the whites believed themselves to be in danger of
losing their electoral majority could petition the legislature for an
act imposing an additional requirement that voters own property
worth $250; that act would apply only to the county that petitioned
for it. As this had never yet been deemed necessary, the suffragists
had a hard time believing white supremacy to be in jeopardy.

Indeed, the suffragists saw white supremacy as a bogus issue.
Lila Meade Valentine, who was president of the Equal Suffrage
League, called it "nonsense," "the last stand of the antis." The novelist Mary Johnston said much the same thing. "If it wasn't the
Negro woman (poor soul!), it would be something else—anything
or everything—farfetchedness wouldn't matter." Farfetchedness, as
we shall see, indeed did not matter to the antis. It did matter to the
suffragists, though. They continued to wrap themselves in the constitution and to insist in moderate tones that race was not an issue.
That was their position, both in their public pronouncements and in
their private correspondence with one another.

In 1916 the suffrage amendment was brought before the legislature a third time. This time it did relatively well, losing in the house
by a vote of forty to fifty-two. I do not know why it did so well—the
suffragists *themselves* were surprised—but it may have been due in
part to the suffragists' own very diligent district-by-district organizing. In national terms, the movement was picking up steam, having
added six states to the woman suffrage column since 1912, and having also emerged as a high-energy, highly visible mass movement.

In any case the legislative session of 1916 was the first in which antisuffrage legislators brought out the heavy artillery, claiming that every argument for woman suffrage was an argument for universal suffrage, that "equal suffrage rights would mean equal race rights," that all of these things would lead to the downfall of civilization. (The antis were very fond of prophesying the downfall of civilization.) The gentleman who led the charge here also added that in woman suffrage states, women had wrinkles and hawklike faces. (There is a certain style of oratorical buffoonery here that I would like to understand better.) Prosuffrage legislators came back with their usual measured response.

Forty to fifty-two was the best woman suffrage would ever do in Virginia (at least until 1952, when the legislature at last roused itself and ratified the Nineteenth Amendment). Woman suffrage did not come before the general assembly again until 1919, and by that time a great deal had changed. There was the war, of course, a red scare, a season of deadly racial violence, and a surge of hope for a new world order. All of this provided more material for the suffrage debates. There was also a shift of emphasis within the suffrage movement itself from campaigns for state constitutional amendments to a final massive, disciplined push for the federal amendment, also called the Anthony Amendment. The Virginia suffragists quietly put aside their state amendment, and threw in their lot with the national movement for the Anthony Amendment. Nothing could have made the antis happier, for here was an opportunity to divert discussion away from the issue of women voting and to stand instead on the hallowed ground of states' rights.

Why the suffragists were willing to go with the federal amendment is something of a mystery. They may have thought that Virginia women would never get the vote any other way; the framers of the 1902 Virginia constitution had deliberately made it very difficult to amend that constitution. Another possible explanation is that the suffragists were basically a cosmopolitan lot, and this, more than any factor like social class, is what separated them from the antis. The suffragists saw themselves as part of a national movement, indeed a global movement, of activist women and progressive male allies who were out to remake the world.

In any case, they threw in with the national suffrage movement, they championed the federal amendment—and they got skewered.

The antis painted the federal amendment as an unconscionable violation of states' rights: states' rights were the foundation not only of southern civilization but also of liberty, democracy, and American government. The foundation of states' rights in turn was the power of each state to determine the character of its electorate. Therefore, any federal amendment affecting the electorate in the states was a threat to liberty, democracy, the principles of American government, and civilization itself (there goes civilization again).

Not surprisingly, the antis also hitched the states' rights issue explicitly to anxieties about white supremacy. Now the Anthony Amendment did not directly enfranchise anyone; like the Fifteenth Amendment, its phrasing was negative, stating that citizens could not be denied the right to vote on the basis of sex. It also empowered Congress to enforce that principle. Antis with any regard for reason therefore had to phrase their argument with some care. And the careful argument was this: if the federal government was allowed to interfere with the state's power to define its electorate in one way, it might be more likely to interfere with the state's power in yet other ways. It might, for example, opt for enforcement of the Fifteenth Amendment (which denies states the power to deny citizens the vote on the basis of race). The careful argument was that one thing might lead to another.

Not that most antis were careful. By 1919 the *Times-Dispatch* was claiming that the Anthony Amendment would directly enfranchise millions of black women, and that it would put an end to segregated schools and to every other form of Jim Crow legislation. As the general assembly prepared to trounce the federal amendment in 1919 and again in 1920, the claims of the antis became outrageous. Not only would woman suffrage mean black political supremacy, but it would bring social equality as well, and it was already responsible for the race riots that racked the country in 1919.

Listen to this newspaper ad that appeared immediately before the legislature prepared to vote on suffrage in 1919: "What causes race riots? In Chicago it was politics. . . . In Washington and Knoxville it was aroused by attacks on women. As a thinking citizen, with an understanding of the laws of cause and effect, you know that race riots will increase if there is more politics between the races and if women are mixed up in politics!"

The antis' behavior was just as trashy as their rhetoric. Carrie

Chapman Catt was the president of the National American Woman Suffrage Association and is routinely chastised by feminist historians for her conservatism and for her obsession with respectability. When Catt went to Richmond to speak to the general assembly about suffrage, she arrived to find the house chamber blanketed with leaflets associating her with miscegenation, atheism, and socialism. The episode degenerated from there.

The suffragists responded to such demagoguery in their usual fashion. They pointed out that even with the federal amendment, the states would retain the right to stipulate qualifications for voters; states' rights would thus be maintained. From there the suffragists rehearsed the standard list of safeguards: the white majorities in most counties, the poll tax, the literacy test.

The suffragists never went much lower than that, even though they had all the chances in the world to try to out-bait the antis. One of the curious things about the antis' position is that they often paid tribute to the potential good citizenship of black women, at the same time belittling black men. An editorial from Newport News reads, "We have managed the men, but could we manage the women? . . . We believe that most of the women would qualify, and we further believe that they would persuade many of the men to qualify; and pay their poll tax for them if need be." An editorial from Winchester contends: "The Negro woman as a rule is ahead of the Negro man. She is the wage-earner and as such has rule over the indolent Negro man. He may stay away from the polls, but she won't." And one antisuffrage legislator claimed that black women would face "twenty-five shotguns" in order to vote. The corollary, of course, was that refined white ladies would not vote, and thus was white supremacy endangered.

Here it seems worthwhile to notice what the suffragists did *not* say in response. Given the antis' claims about the character of black women, the truly expedient course for the suffragists would have been to attack those claims by disparaging the character of black women. But that the suffragists steadfastly refused to do. For all the trouble the race question was giving them in the last two years of the campaign, they never stooped to making mean remarks about black people, either publicly or to one another.

Was it racism that ultimately defeated woman suffrage in Virginia? This question is impossible to answer; if anything in Virginia was ever overdetermined, it was opposition to feminism. A legislative head count suggests that the race issue did indeed help the antis; delegates from heavily black counties were somewhat more likely to vote against woman suffrage than were their colleagues from other parts of the state. At the same time, the legislature was perfectly capable of squashing feminist aspirations when no racial issue was at stake. The campaign for a state-supported college for women coordinated with the University of Virginia had the support of almost every white women's organization in the state, and it went without saying that this college would be for whites only. But it, too, was defeated in one legislative session after another.

What is clear is that the antis were willing to exploit racist arguments for whatever effectiveness they might prove to have. They introduced the race question, and in agitating it they had no standards of minimal decency to which they held themselves or anyone else. And so they controlled the terms of the suffrage debate. As a result, the suffragists were censored to a considerable degree; it was not possible for a suffragist to suggest that significant numbers of blacks might be enfranchised or that enfranchised blacks might do something worthwhile with their votes.

Meanwhile, black Virginians were virtually silenced on the suffrage issue. In the North the great majority of blacks who expressed opinions on the issue were prosuffrage, and it seems reasonable to suppose that southern blacks felt the same way. But given what the antis were up to in Virginia, a black who supported woman suffrage could only damage the cause by saying so. Virginia's black newspapers, and I have read all of them for this period, made only occasional, noncommittal remarks about woman suffrage. As for the opinions of black women, we have nothing but a few tantalizing clues. In 1916 Richmond's black newspaper (the *Planet*) reported on a basketball game played by two teams of black female public school teachers: one team called themselves the Feminists, while the other called themselves the Suffragists.

The Nineteenth Amendment was ratified in 1920, no thanks to Virginia. Once it was ratified, black views of woman suffrage became somewhat clearer. In the biggest cities, registrars were required by law to open up centralized public-registration offices, and under those circumstances black women were able to organize major voter-registration campaigns. In Richmond, more than twenty-four hundred black women registered; by the time the Richmond registrar closed the books, there were as many black women as black men registered. (The 2,410 women equaled 12.5 percent of black women aged twenty-one and older; the 2,402 men equaled 14.8 percent. White women registrants were outnumbered by white men by almost three to one, 28,148 to 10,645. The white male percentage was 79.4, while the white female percentage was 26.8.)

The Richmond situation also beams us back on the fact that much of the story about woman suffrage and white supremacy lies less in the suffrage movement than in the Democratic machine. Black women in Richmond had to wait for hours to register because the registrar would provide only one person to work the desk. Maggie Walker, the African American banker and insurance executive registrar, took the registrar to court to get the proceedings speeded up, but there were still cases of black women who waited all day and were sent home without having registered when the shop was closed for the night.

What's more, when the Democratic politicians in Richmond saw those long lines of African American women, they got worried. First they sent out urgent appeals to their lieutenants all over the state to get conservative white women registered. Second, once registration was complete and everyone refocused on the election itself, the Democrats tried to discipline the new women voters by announcing that anyone who failed to vote a straight Democratic ticket would be barred from voting in the following year's Democratic primary. (Of course, the primary was the real election.)

Meanwhile, the situation was quite different in small towns and in the countryside. There, all the registrar had to do to keep a black woman from voting was to pretend not to be home. It is not clear what the precise combination of factors was, but in the rural counties registration figures for black women were usually low: 3 percent, 1 percent, zero. (When I say 3 percent I mean that 3 percent of the county's total adult black female population was registered.) So far I have managed to scrounge registration figures from ten counties. The pattern that seems to be developing is this: Black registration was lowest (under 4 percent) where there were lots of Democrats and a high proportion of blacks in the population. Black registration was higher—up to 21 percent—in cities and also in counties where there was a vital Republican organization or a low percentage of black people in the overall population.

As for the white suffrage activists, some of them turned out to be in the vanguard of liberalism, at least by the standard of the times. As the first election day approached, some of the Richmond suffragists became concerned that election officials might try to stop black women from voting, and that there might be violence. They invited several black women community leaders to a meeting to discuss strategy (the meeting was held on white turf, in the studio of Adele Clark and Nora Houston—since they were artists they thought they could pull off this daring stunt and have it chalked up to artistic eccentricity). It was agreed that the white women would cruise the polling places the next day to make sure there was no trouble. A half dozen white suffragists fulfilled this promise the next day, and, as Clark told it later, black women were able to vote without incident.

Some further evidence emerged in the early 1920s, when black and white liberal leaders of both sexes came together to launch Virginia's first interracial movement. Among the white women who pledged themselves to work for interracial cooperation, at least a third were former suffrage activists.

In trying to recontextualize the arguments about woman suffrage and white supremacy, I realize I have composed something of a moral tale, with the antis firmly entrenched as the bad guys. I am not trying to cast the suffragists by contrast in a heroic role. They did not *challenge* white supremacy, and because they were political outsiders they never had to face certain tough decisions: *Should* there be restrictions on who votes? If so, what should they be? Since the framers of the constitution of 1902 had already done that dirty work, the suffragists were excused from it. The white suffragists did *not* include African Americans in their democratic vision, and it is important that we continue to mark that fact so that history can serve its ongoing function as social criticism and, for feminists, self-criticism.

But having cast the antis as bad guys, I would still cast the suffragists as not-so-bad, and there is an analytic point here, as well as a moral judgment: that bad and not-so-bad are worth distinguishing from one another. Racism, as Barbara Fields has argued, is not one single entity. Its character changes depending on who is using it against whom; it is institutionalized in different ways in different times and places; its consequences are variable; its intensity is a matter of degree. Those distinctions were critical to black Virginians; the black press in this period makes it very clear that black editors made those distinctions all the time, and perhaps they should be just as important in our historical analysis.

As we try to see racism as this more variable entity, I think it also makes sense to see expediency as a variable entity, and here I want to suggest that we recast our thinking about the relationships between expediency, racism, and feminism. It is true, as Aileen Kraditor argued twenty-five years ago, that there were some feminists who found it expedient to exploit anxieties about white supremacy. Kate Gordon of Louisiana, who was Kraditor's star witness, is probably the best example. But I am arguing that, in Virginia anyhow, it was the antis who used racism in a thoroughly expedient way. For the suffragists there were both external and internal limits on the degree to which the racism was used to advance the woman suffrage cause. When I say that there were external limits, I mean that in the end racism was a scourge to feminism. When all was said and done, in those states where white supremacy was a major obsession, woman suffrage failed. Feminism could have gone further and accomplished more had it not been for the bigotry that ran deeper in conservative politicians and the white population as a whole than it did in suffragists.

Of course, the white suffragists themselves may not have seen it that way in 1912 or 1918. Nevertheless, in Virginia the white suffragists placed limits on themselves in terms of how deeply expedient they would allow themselves to be. As I have argued already, they did not resort to race baiting—which, remember, was commonplace in white male political practice—nor did they pander to white supremacist thinking by proposing that there be special restrictions on *female* voters, restrictions that would virtually eliminate the black female vote. As early as 1913, the leaders of the suffrage league did pause to consider whether they themselves ought to propose such special restrictions. The novelist Mary Johnston wrote to the Equal Suffrage League's president, Lila Meade Valentine, arguing that they should not offer a novel set of restrictions: "I think that as women we should be most prayerfully careful lest, in the future, women—whether coloured women or white women who are merely poor—should be able to say that we had betrayed their interests and excluded them from freedom."

So when woman suffrage came to Virginia by action of the other states, it was at least not a setback for blacks. In fact, in some respects, it was the first step forward in decades. The size of the black electorate was doubled. For a few thousand black women it opened the door to the dignity of citizenship; it gave them a new means of resistance; and it offered to a select few a voice in national political councils, chiefly through the Republican Party. For black Virginians woman suffrage did not bring democracy in any absolute sense. But it did move in a democratic direction, which is more than you can say for anything else in Virginia politics for a period of many decades.

Sex and the Sectional Conflict

November 1990
New Orleans, Louisiana

Sectional conflict is a topic that has long dominated interpretations of political culture in antebellum America.[1] Equally powerful in the past quarter century has been the notion that men and women defined themselves or were confined to separate spheres by a growing body of prescriptive literature pouring forth during the early national era. North and South as well as masculine and feminine have endured as both meaningful divides and significant ideological constructions for understanding the American past.

But in some ways these systems of thought, these ways of viewing difference, have remained in separate compartments without any sense of their interconnection—at least in the public political discourse of the antebellum era. Certainly, gender conventions influenced political leaders when they made their arguments in the press and on the platform. Many of these male orators were skilled at employing symbols of masculinity to enhance their own roles and barbs of femininity to diminish their detractors. Further, sexual innuendo often interacted with political bombast. With struggle, we can begin to decode and incorporate issues of sexuality into our appreciations of our past. Presidential among other politics are now

1. I want to thank Ken Greenberg, Jean Baker, LeeAnn Whites, and especially William Freehling for comments on early drafts. I would also like to thank the Douglas Southall Freeman Professorship for its generous support of my scholarship.

CATHERINE CLINTON

43

being revised in light of our reckoning with these crucial factors. The time seems ripe for exploring questions involving the sexual politics of sectional conflict.

Certainly, there is no way to demonstrate that North and South created separate sexual norms and behaviors, nor any need to. But there is tantalizing evidence to indicate a biracial slave society emphasized and exaggerated patterns and ideologies that profoundly affected sexual relations within southern society. These distinctions did not constitute a fundamentally different social construction, but a viable distinction was nonetheless produced as a result of the South's "peculiar institution."

Within the Old South, a system of gender behavior emerged that was not merely modeled on the patriarchy of colonial forebears. Within plantation society, patriarchs considered themselves as keepers of a more sacred flame. Patterns developed in ancient Greece that shaped the self-consciousness of the slave-owner class. Some classical scholars have labeled this cultural ideal a "phallocracy." At the same time, slave owners of the early national era paid deliberative homage to the Roman Republic, loving tributes that ranged from their taking Roman pseudonyms on political tracts to naming slaves Cato and Cicero. For the purposes of the Old South, perhaps the term *penarchy* is more appropriate, a deliberate bastardization, a mix of Latin and Greek.

Penarchy identifies a syndrome whereby males of the elite use sexual coercion and force *in addition* to economic and political oppression to control women in both subordinate and dominant classes, *as well as a means to control all other men.* In essence, the term sexualizes patriarchy and incorporates notions of race and class into its systematic refinement of power relations, in much the way the Roman Republic classified status in terms of gender, citizenship, and rigidly defined characteristics. Penarchy can be a useful analytical tool in investigating almost all colonial cultures, from imperial India to the Ottoman rule on the North African coast, to the Spanish and Portuguese settlements throughout the New World, and most certainly to the planter regime in the Old South.

Those of us working on the Old South are sensitized that labels and definitions constitute divisions. The divide between lady and woman was significant—not unlike the status ranking of free black and slave. By thinking in terms of penarchy we can see how status is sexualized, and linked to power relationships within society. Indeed, sexual identity cannot be *encoded* without a specific cultural context of power and status. Penarchy automatically includes class or race considerations without isolating and, in a sense, privileging gender.

On antebellum southern plantations the rituals of enslavement sometimes were sexualized and almost always reflected penarchal values. Slave men and women were subject to physical restraints, many with implicitly sexual overtones: collars, cuffs, ropes, and other icons of submission. Slaves frequently were subjected to public nudity; one of the first laws of racial differentiation in the Virginia colony was that white indentured servants might not be stripped for punishment. Whipping itself was an extension of male will, masculine power—and lashing can suggest a form of sexual sublimation.

Slave owners wanted to maintain absolute power and control over their slaves. Many of these interactions were about not simply control, but the salacious and prurient interests of those empowered. Elizabeth Keckley recalled a humiliating experience when a member of her master's church wanted to whip her, without cause. She resisted and commented: "Recollect I was eighteen years of age, was a woman fully developed and yet this man coolly bade me take down my dress."[2] An enormous amount of rich material and unexplored subtexts emerges if historians redirect their energies with empathy rather than hostility toward sexualized rereadings of the past.

Many of the texts and certainly the textures surrounding sectional conflicts were charged with gender and sexuality. The language of orators and authors, the metaphors employed, the embattlement of actual men and women within competing movements present a rich storehouse of material for exploring these new avenues.

During one of the first congressional imbroglios over slavery, none other than James Madison, Federalist First Father and a slave-owning patriarch, put pen to paper to capture the tensions of the time. Shortly after the Missouri Compromise, Madison composed a

2. Elizabeth Keckley, *Behind the Scenes* (New York: Oxford University Press, 1988), 33.

"fable."[3] This was such an abbreviated and fanciful tale that he did not publish the piece until 1835. One Madison scholar has called this thirteen-page document a "whimsical flight of fancy," yet anyone interested in slavery, sexuality, or the sectional conflict will find this tale riveting.

Madison wrote within a popular genre of the day. Jonathan and Mary Bull were the descendants of old John Bull, and they married to unite against their common ancestor. They were fruitful and multiplied, but somewhere between their tenth and eleventh child, conflict erupted. Jonathan became unreasonable in his conduct toward his beloved wife. He reproached her for the infirmity they both suffered as children. His flecks of black had faded, while the stain on his wife's left arm grew. This symbol of African slavery, Madison wrote, drove Bull to taunt his wife and insist "she should, if the color could not be taken out, either tear off the skin from the flesh, or cut off the limb." Well over half this pamphlet contains Mary's response. Writing a "fable" may have given the author freer rein to express himself.

Madison argued that Jonathan "looked at the black arm, and forgot all the rest," the happy union, the ten children, the shared fear of John Bull. Mary responded: "When you talk of tearing off the skin, or cutting off the unfortunate limb, must I remind you, of what you cannot be ignorant, that the most skillful surgeons have given their opinions that if so cruel an operation were to be tried, it could hardly fail to be followed by a mortification, or a bleeding to death?" The language of the pamphlet and of the day did not allow graphic descriptions, but certainly the image conjured was repellent. Mary herself comments, "Should neither of the fatal effects ensue, you would like me better in my mangled or mutilated condition than you do now?" As the quarrel winds down, Madison allows "good heart, steady temper, sound head" to triumph, and "the bickering which had sprung up ended, as the quarrels of lovers *always*, and of married folks *sometimes* do, in an increased affection and confidence between parties." Madison's happy ending did not prevail in real life, nor ironically in fiction, as Nathaniel Hawthorne's 1843 story "The Birthmark" confronts a similar theme.

3. I am indebted to Robert Allison of Suffolk University for bringing this piece to my attention (*Virginia Magazine of History and Biography* 99:3 [July 1991]: 327–50).

In Hawthorne's version, the husband, a scientist, plots to rid himself of his wife's single physical blight. He worries, yet his wife exclaims: "Danger? There is but one danger—that this horrible stigma shall be left upon my cheek! Remove it, remove it whatever be the cost!" She gulps down his experimental potion, her crimson imperfection fades, but "the parting breath of the new perfect woman passed into the atmosphere, and her soul, lingering a moment near her husband took its heavenward flight." Simultaneously, the blemish is gone, the body purified.

Hawthorne's tale does not hint at slavery, although we know that his contacts with abolitionist circles were extensive. Further, the "stain of slavery" rhetoric was widely employed at the time, so his language may have been influenced by his intellectual circle. Hawthorne's work dealt extensively and explicitly with the sexual politics of his day. And, as Jean Yellin suggests, Hester Prynne's *A* in *The Scarlet Letter* may symbolize more than her colonial sins— perhaps it is a premonition of the tribulations of her great-grand-daughter's generation.[4] Certainly, the Grimké sisters lived up to this forecast. They alienated their Carolina family by turning their backs on slavery, and scandalized their northern listeners by addressing "promiscuous" audiences—a suggestive phrasing. If Prynne's *A* even subconsciously stood also for abolitionism, many of the scenes in which the woman outside her designated sphere is trapped by the mob blend nicely with the moral universe Hawthorne was in as well as the one that he created.

Hawthorne provides a tragic ending, but Madison provides no ending at all. His light closing cannot divert us from unresolved issues: Would Jonathan have forced the operation, perceiving Mary as his property? Could Jonathan tolerate Mary's arm once he became fixated? Consequently, would their union disintegrate? Would he have loved her as an amputee? Was divorce inevitable? Did all this bloody symbolism prefigure maiming and mayhem along the border, in the sorrowful state of Kansas, "Bloody Kansas"?

Significantly, Madison's tale would be one of the few times that the South would be feminized by a southern statesman until John

4. See Jean Yellin, *Women and Sisters* (New Haven: Yale University Press, 1990).

Brown's invasion—when "she" required protection from Yankee attack. Perhaps at the time of the tale's publication, the South felt it had successfully fought off gender advances promoted by the gelded North. As the witches and harpies of Yankee abolitionism spawned their women's rights movement, the South silenced them in the national forum with the gag rule in Congress. Proslavery forces outmaneuvered their abolitionist counterpart all the way up to the Supreme Court with the Dred Scott decision in 1857. Madison was willing, from this position of increasing strength, to propose the South as Mary Bull, a southern lady in distress: her single stain due to no fault of her own.

The outcry over Missouri in 1819 hinted at the disharmony to follow; the clashing of symbols became common practice for debates between North and South. Within plantation worlds, masculine and feminine were exaggerated not just for effect, but to distinguish genteel civilization from the horrors found within the modernizing North. The specter of women in factories, women in schoolrooms, and women attending—a lot less addressing—public meetings set off alarm bells in the South. Clearly, gender roles were increasingly blurred among the Yankees. No such gender blending polluted plantation culture, and even sharper divisions emerged in response. Fire-eaters saluted frail flowers of femininity and projected models of masculinity uncomfortably close to caricature.[5]

Southerners struggled to corner the market on martial virtue, cultivating honor codes, which included caning, dueling, whipping, general bullying, as well as sexual license. The penarchy thrived and despised what it perceived as a pathetic counterculture in the North: a *mammarchy* that fostered the warm, nurturing, softening influence of female reformers.

The rise of a northern antislavery counterculture has been dealt with in innumerable studies. Biographies of individual leaders, studies of the reform crusade, and portraits of black abolitionists and women abolitionists (even a new study of black women abolitionists) all continue to pour forth.[6] None label abolitionist culture

5. This near nonsensical quality is best captured in the several scenes where men provoke one another to duels in the plantation epic *Jezebel* (1938).
6. See Lewis Perry and Michael Fellman, eds., *Abolitionism Reconsidered* (Baton Rouge: Louisiana State University Press, 1979); Robert Abzug, *Passionate Liberator:*

mammarchy, although social histories and biographical studies lay the groundwork for this interpretation.

Very few scholars are prepared for this kind of sexualized, sectional vocabulary. Bertram Wyatt-Brown, in his thoughtful essays in *Yankee Saints and Southern Sinners*, continues his strong case for fundamental cultural divides begun three years earlier in *Southern Honor: Ethics and Behavior in the Old South*. Wyatt-Brown writes instructively about southern character: "The identification of the individual with his blood relations, his community, his state, and whatever other associations the *man of honor* [emphasis added] feels are important for establishing his claim for recognition. . . . " Linda Kerber, in her article "Women and Individualism in American History," suggests: "The language of individualism as it developed in antebellum America was not a woman's language. How could it be? It was a trope whose major theme was the denial of dependence." Kerber goes on to point out that this language of individualism from the antebellum era onward "has been a male-centered discourse, that its imagery has traditionally served the self-interest of men, whatever their class."[7]

Moving from the individual to the collective, Wyatt-Brown is most persuasive on the topic of sectionalism and its discontents:

> As a result, the lawyer and the politician were powerful figures not only in governmental affairs but in ethical concerns of society as well. That *breed of men* [emphasis added] was to the South what philanthropists and evangelical ministers were to the North: models of public morality and sectional ideology. As the latter group became increasingly optimistic about human good

---

Theodore Dwight Weld and the Dilemma of Reform (New York: Oxford University Press, 1980); Dorothy Sterling, *Ahead of Her Time: Abby Kelley and the Politics of Antislavery* (New York: W. W. Norton, 1991); Lawrence J. Friedman, *Gregarious Saints* (New York: Cambridge University Press, 1982); James B. Stewart, *Holy Warriors* (New York: Hill and Wang, 1976); Benjamin Quarles, *Black Abolitionists* (New York: Oxford University Press, 1969); Jane H. Pease and William H. Pease, *They Who Would Be Free: Blacks' Search for Freedom* (New York: Atheneum, 1974); Blanche Hersch, *The Slavery of Sex* (Urbana: University of Illinois Press, 1986); Yellin, *Women and Sisters;* and Shirley Yee, *Black Women Abolitionists* (Knoxville: University of Tennessee Press, 1992).

7. Bertram Wyatt-Brown, *Yankee Saints and Southern Sinners* (Baton Rouge: Louisiana State University Press, 1985), 186; Linda Kerber, "Women and Individualism," *Massachusetts Review* 30:4 (winter 1989): 600, 606.

and public progress, the former watched the moral change with growing dread.[8]

Ann Douglas in her influential study of 1977, *The Feminization of American Culture*, demonstrated the ways in which northern female reformers usurped male prerogative during this era, sharing the spotlight with those "feminized" philanthropists and ministers.

When female abolitionists called a women's convention in New York in 1837, after repeated conflicts within the antislavery leadership as well as the rank and file concerning women's role in the movement, newspapers satirized their efforts:

> Yes, most unbelieving reader, it is a fact of most ludicrous solemnity, that "our female brethren" have been lifting up their voices. The spinster has thrown aside her distaff—the blooming beauty her guitar—the matron her darning needle—the sweet novelist her crow-quill; the young mother has left her baby to nestle alone in the cradle—and the kitchen maid her pots and frying pans—to discuss the weighty matters of state—to decide upon intricate questions of international policy.[9]

This was a lame response compared to the mob attack on the women's convention in 1838 in Philadelphia, but nevertheless demonstrated deep pockets of venom that characterized sectional politics. When women stepped outside their "proper," private spheres—especially to traipse onto the sacred ground of proslavery politics—penarchs foamed with rage and, since few could contain their Pavlovian response, shouted "Harlot!"

Abolitionist Maria Weston Chapman realized that it was sometimes better to meet ridicule with satire, and she sometimes penned barbed responses to male rage:

> "They've taken a notion to speak for themselves,
>   And are wielding the tongue and the pen;
>   They've mounted the rostrum; the termagant elves,
>   and—oh horrid!—are talking to men!"

Lucretia Mott, Maria Weston Chapman, L. Maria Child, and Abby Kelley were instrumental in "feminizing" the mass move-

---

8. Wyatt-Brown, *Yankee Saints and Southern Sinners*, 216.
9. Sterling, *Ahead of Her Time*, 50.

ment opposing slavery. Kelley broke with her Quaker faith to maintain her activist role. Maria Chapman argued, "Women, whose efforts for the cause could not be hindered by men, were more valuable auxiliaries than the men whose dignity forbade them to be fellow laborers with women."[10] The debates over women's roles and the harm their contributions might do to the antislavery cause split the Boston organizations in the winter of 1839-1840. Following this crisis, women's participation in antislavery rallies was sexualized. In the spring of 1840 when Abby Kelley attended the Connecticut Anti-Slavery annual meeting in New Haven, the floor of the convention was flooded with acrimony. One clergyman declared:

> No woman will speak or vote where I am moderator. It is enough for women to rule at home. It is woman's business to take care of the children in the nursery; she has no business to come into this meeting and by speaking and voting lord it over men. Where woman's enticing eloquence is heard, men are incapable of right and efficient action. She beguiles and blinds men by her smiles and her bland winning voice. . . . I will not sit in a meeting where the sorcery of a woman's tongue is thrown around my heart. I will not submit to a PETTICOAT GOVERNMENT.[11]

"Smiles" and "winning voice" were direct references to Eve and the fall of man. This antislavery advocate, perhaps as much as a proslavery man, feared an articulate Eve as much as any serpent. All women were denied the right to speak and vote for the remainder of the two-day meeting.

Those men who were unwilling to abandon female equality formed a radical core—a handful of antislavery activitists. Championing women's equality was a goal to which many antislavery advocates rallied. Elizabeth Cady Stanton explained the case for an alliance between women and people of color: "For while the man is born to do whatever he can, for the woman and the negro there is no such privilege. There is a Procrustean bedstead ever ready for them, body and soul, and all mankind stands on alert to restrain their

10. G. B. Barker-Benfield and Catherine Clinton, eds., *Portraits of American Women* (New York: Oxford University Press, 1998), 160.
11. Sterling, *Ahead of Her Time*, 108–9.

impulses, check their aspirations, fetter their limbs, lest, in their freedom and strength, in their full development, they should take an even platform with the proud man himself."[12]

Whether she intended it or not, Stanton was stepping onto explosive terrain. She was juxtaposing the black (who was always masculinized) with the woman (who was always identified as white) in a bed, however procrustean. Indeed, this very image was a bludgeon employed not only by southern men but also by northern men to keep antislavery women on the defense. In 1839 when 785 "ladies of Lynn" petitioned the Massachusetts legislature "to repeal all laws which make any distinction amongst its inhabitants, on account of color," the press followed the lead of the lawmakers and debased the matter to these women seeking "the privilege of marrying black husbands."[13] (It took four years to repeal the law.)

Despite these direct confrontations with the legislature, with the pulpit, and with many other aspects of public life, women's rights advocates nevertheless managed to agitate and resist throughout this particularly rich period of reform. Gender and sexuality provided explosive undercurrents. Symbols of masculinity and femininity were bandied about in headlines, political cartoons, and stump speeches; they were woven into the fabric of American political culture. Petticoats and hoopskirts were weaponry used to diminish opponents.[14]

An impressive body of scholarship that lays the foundation for a fresh interpretation of antebellum sectional conflict may be found in the work of Ronald Walters.[15] Walters pioneered a path more than a decade ago, detecting a specific genre of abolitionist vituperation—the "sinning South." The antislavery advocates—through their own tone and language—projected an image of slave owners, which

12. Catherine Clinton, *The Other Civil War: American Women in the Nineteenth Century* (New York: Hill and Wang, 1984), 70.

13. Sterling, *Ahead of Her Time*, 78–79.

14. See, for example, Clinton, *The Other Civil War*, 14–16; and Nina Silber, "Intemperate Men, Spiteful Women, and Jefferson Davis," in *Divided Houses: Gender and the Civil War*, ed. Catherine Clinton and Nina Silber (New York: Oxford University Press, 1992), 283–305.

15. See Ronald G. Walters, *The Anti-Slavery Appeal: American Abolitionism after 1830* (Baltimore: Johns Hopkins University Press, 1978), and Ronald G. Walters, *American Reformers, 1815–1860* (New York: Hill and Wang, 1978).

they themselves sexualized.[16] Walters's very rich and powerful analysis of this "erotic South" remains relatively unchallenged, either by critics or by supporters, despite the vast outpouring of research on reform.

The antebellum South hoarded symbols of virility in its debates with Yankee opponents.[17] Slave owners reckoned the manly image of their northern rivals paled by comparison with southern frontier heroes—half wielding an ax and the other half wielding the whip. No episode in antebellum history so vividly captures this dramatic sexualization of sectional divide more than the Sumner-Brooks confrontation of 1856, an episode that ironically eclipsed John Brown's volcanic debut.

By 1856 sectional tensions had ridden roughshod over parliamentary politeness in Congress—the Compromise Congress: the Compromise of 1850, the Kansas-Nebraska Act of 1854, and the raging debates over "popular sovereignty" eroded whatever civilities had reigned on Capitol Hill. But nothing really prepared lawmakers for the outburst of violence on the Senate floor in the wake of Sen. Charles Sumner's "Crime against Kansas" speech.

The Massachusetts senator was a well-known antislavery advocate who had long pleaded to let freedom ring. A Harvard-educated crusading lawyer, Sumner had argued for integrated schools in the landmark Roberts versus Boston case in 1849. He was a founder of the Free-Soil Party in 1848, and joined with the Republicans in 1855. In the spring of 1856 he composed and delivered one of the most important speeches of his career. The five-hour oration, begun on May 19, was carefully prepared, and Sumner had hundreds of copies printed for distribution on the second and concluding day of his speech, May 20. "The Crime against Kansas" was a masterful summation of southern wrongs and northern rights obstructed. The address also contained personal attacks on several Senate colleagues. Most particularly, he savaged an elderly gentleman from South Carolina, Sen. Andrew Butler, who was absent from the floor

16. Ronald G. Walters, "The Erotic South: Civilization and Sexuality in American Abolitionism," *American Quarterly* 25 (1973): 177–201.

17. On this issue, Wyatt-Brown has been most eloquent in both *Southern Honor* and *Yankee Saints and Southern Sinners.*

during Sumner's diatribe. However, Preston Brooks, a cousin of Butler's who served in the House of Representatives, witnessed Sumner's aspersions.

In a particularly slanderous double entendre, Sumner called Butler the "Don Quixote of slavery . . . who has chose a mistress to whom he has made his vows, and who, though ugly to others, is always lovely to him; though polluted in the sight of the world, is chaste in his sight . . . the harlot, Slavery."[18] This attack was a thinly veiled reference to hypocritical slaveholders who preached racial purity while fathering mulattoes. This was considered an especially low blow in light of the fact that Butler had no such reputation. His fellow senators found this characterization vicious. (It was far more appropriate for the next senator from South Carolina, James Henry Hammond, who was sent to Washington in 1857.)

Sumner's speech aroused passions. One Tennessee congressman remarked after the first day: "Mr. Sumner ought to be knocked down, and his face jumped into."[19] Preston Brooks, also an elected representative of the Palmetto State, was thrown into a frenzy; he plotted his revenge. He waited until May 21 when he could read a copy of the text before he decided to act. Brooks took the prescribed path dictated by southern honor: he would not bother to "call Sumner out." Dueling was outlawed, Sumner would refuse such a challenge, and Brooks did not want to tip his hand. Further, the Code Duello warned that gentlemen should not risk their lives in contests with unworthy opponents—thus, offenders beneath the rank of gentleman might be caned or horsewhipped instead.

On May 22, not long after noon, after the Senate had adjourned, Brooks approached Sumner's desk and said: "Mr. Sumner, I have read your speech twice over carefully. It is a libel on South Carolina, and Mr. Butler, who is a relative of mine. . . ."[20] Brooks began to strike Sumner on the head with his gold-tipped cane before Sumner could respond. Indeed, he trapped him in his seat, and Sumner was forced to tear the desk from its moorings in an effort to escape. Sumner sustained nearly thirty blows that took Brooks perhaps less than

18. David Herbert Donald, *Charles Sumner and the Coming of the Civil War* (New York: Alfred A. Knopf, 1960), 285.

19. Ibid., 289.

20. Ibid., 294. In some versions, Brooks says "a friend of mine," in others he has much more to say; see Donald's footnote on the discrepancies.

a minute to administer. Brooks beat Sumner savagely before stalking out, unimpeded. Sumner was soaked in his own blood, knocked senseless, and gravely injured—he would not return to his desk for more than two years.

This news of violence on the floor of the Senate electrified the country. The clashing interpretations of honor and virtue echoed throughout the land. As David Donald described in his authoritative *Charles Sumner and the Coming of the Civil War*, rallies to Sumner's cause were held throughout the North.[21] Not just abolitionist agitators, but ordinary citizens seemed moved by this event. George Templeton Strong wrote in his diary: "News tonight that Charles Sumner of the Senate has been licked by a loaded cane by a certain honorable Carolinian Brooks for his recent rather sophomorical anti-slavery speech. I hold the anti-slavery agitators wrong in principle and mischievous in policy. But the reckless, insolent brutality of our Southern aristocrats may drive me into abolitionism yet."[22]

Brooks's affair of honor, heralded in the southern press, exacerbated congressional tension. Following Brooks's conviction of assault charges, Congress voted 121 for and 95 against expulsion. As it was not the two-thirds required to turn him out, Brooks claimed "vindication" and took the opportunity to make a speech in the House of Representatives on July 14. Boastful and arrogant, Brooks called one opponent a "feminine gentleman," another a "poltroon and a puppy" who was "a cock that crows and won't fight, despised by the hens and even by the pullets." He theatrically announced his resignation and "walking out of the House was met at the door by Southern women who embraced and kissed him."[23] South Carolina promptly reelected him.

This sequence of events shows the tinderbox atmosphere surrounding sectional conflict. Brooks was painted as a beast by Sumner sympathizers, the stand-in for all the proslavery brutes invading and violating free territories. Sumner represented the voice of reason, northern virtue, and indeed innocence bruised and bashed by southern passion. Sumner as "assault victim" was a clear

21. Ibid., 300.
22. Ibid., 299.
23. Edward L. Pierce, ed., *Memoir and Letters of Charles Sumner* (Boston: Roberts Brothers, 1894), 3:491.

subtext of his emblematic "empty chair" during the crucial years leading up to the war.

Brooks symbolized to the South an active, yearning manhood, a laurel necessarily earned in combat, for how can it be genuine until proved.[24] Brooks's attack upon Sumner served as notice that the South would resort to violence to defend its honor, with reckless disregard for circumstances and surrounding. The Union, states' rights advocates kept reminding northern meddlers, was not sacred. The North stood aghast, both at the attack and at Brooks's subsequent popularity. His cane became a fetish, copied to symbolize southern (white) chauvinism. His name has become a trademark: replicas of his cane are hawked in advertisements, found recently in the pages of the *New Yorker*.

While Sumner's martyrdom and Brooks's celebrity were being fought out in public forums, another sensational sectional conflict exploded. Ironically, this chain of events, which propelled John Brown out of Kansas and into warrior/terrorist status, was almost simultaneous with eruptions on Capitol Hill. Nevertheless, there is no historical evidence to indicate that the two events were linked, as communications did not spread the word of Sumner's attack (which occurred first) until after the infamous "Sack of Lawrence." Nevertheless, W. E. B. Dubois exploited this link imaginatively in his study of Brown when he wrote of the border warfare: "Snatching thus the whip-hand, with proslavery governor, judges, marshal and legislature, they then proceeded in 1855 to deliver blow upon blow to the free state cause until it seemed inevitable that Kansas should become a slave state. . . ."

Hero and martyr, madman and assassin, many labels have been attached to the magnetic historical figure John Brown. He has certainly *not* been portrayed as a sex symbol; yet, the image of John Brown and the vast body of work surrounding sectional conflict during the years leading up to the Civil War suggest a wide range of interpretations involving gender and sexuality. The very language of sectional conflict was informed by sexual hysteria: the "Crimes against Kansas," the "Rape of Kansas," and "outrage at Harpers Ferry." Were the participants in these debates self-

---

24. In Brooks's several accounts, he always remarked that Sumner was physically the larger of the two men, introducing some sort of David and Goliath motif.

conscious about the emotions they tapped with their provocative imagery? Were they simply submerged in the gendered vocabularies that consumed their political culture, unaware of the sexual tensions they exploited? And what was Brown's role in all of this? Was he not the paramount symbol of violation that drove southern whites into a frenzy? Was he not the avenging abolitionist whites secretly feared in the North and openly vilified in the South? He was certainly adopted by African Americans, from Harriet Tubman, who embraced him during his lifetime, to W. E. B. Dubois, whose 1909 biography celebrated this legendary figure, down to Malcolm X, who paid tribute to this singular white hero as well. But what was his role in the larger context of sectional debates and those sexualized wars of words during the decades preceding the outbreak of war?

Kansas was a powder keg in the 1850s.[25] John Brown, the eccentric and obstinate abolitionist, made an auspicious debut. During this period, southern rituals of shame visited antislavery victims regularly. In the summer of 1855, William Phillips, a free-state lawyer from Leavenworth, had been ordered out of the territory. When he failed to leave, Phillips was kidnapped to Missouri, where one side of his head was shaved. Next he was stripped of his clothes, tarred, ridden on the rails, then sold at public auction for one dollar. The proslavery paper *Squatter Sovereign* declared: "We will continue to tar and feather, drown, lynch and hang every white-livered Abolitionist who dares to pollute our soil."[26]

John Brown joined his sons on October 7, 1855, in the Kansas Territory at Osawatomie, near Pottawatomie Creek, which soon became known as Brown's Station. He had a long career of failure behind him. In response to the Fugitive Slave Law in 1850, Brown organized the "United States League of Gileadites." His utopia, christened Gilead, never materialized.[27] Despite his constitution (which granted men and women equality) and his invigorating directives to fellow Gileadites (exhorting them with the example of

25. See James Rawley, *Race and Politics: "Bleeding Kansas" and the Coming of the Civil War* (Philadelphia: Temple University Press, 1969).

26. Jules Abels, *Man on Fire: John Brown and the Cause of Liberty* (New York: Macmillan, 1971), 49.

27. Gilead is also the name Margaret Atwood chose for her fundamentalist future world in *The Handmaid's Tale*, a bizarre coincidence.

the hero of the *Amistad* revolt, Cinque), his proselytizing fell flat and the movement never numbered more than fifty. But Brown's decision to relocate in Kansas, spurred on by New England sponsors, proved fateful.

During a threat of proslavery attacks on Lawrence, Brown and his sons were a formidable sight on December 7—fully armed and their wagon loaded with weaponry. Brown assumed a leadership role in the Kansas Volunteers and drilled his "Liberty Guard," accorded the rank of captain. Combat was avoided, and the Browns retreated back to their settlement. The bitterly cold winter preoccupied most border warriors during the following months.

Later, in the spring of 1856, more than eight hundred Missourians were deputized by a proslavery judge who authorized them to arrest antislavery legislators in Kansas charged with treason. The mob, calling itself a legal posse, entered the town of Lawrence on May 21 and burned two buildings (newspaper offices) to the ground, while a third structure, the Free State Hotel, survived attack. The citizens of Lawrence, unprotected, did little to resist the marauders. When a courier galloped into Brown's Station with news of the siege, John Brown rallied his own troops, the Pottawatomie Rifles. They traveled toward Lawrence, camped out in a ravine, and on May 24 Brown's men moved toward Dutch Henry's Crossing. Near midnight they knocked at the door of a proslavery family named Doyle.

John Doyle, the youngest of three sons, recalled: "They came into the house, handcuffed my father and two older brothers and started to take me, but my mother begged them to leave me as I would be all the protection she would have." This bit of gallantry spared the sixteen year old's life. In daylight, John Doyle found the bodies of his father and brothers, with one brother's fingers cut off. William Sherman, "Dutch Henry's" brother, was also found dead, face down in the creek, his head split open, his left hand severed. Allen Wilkinson, a member of the Shawnee legislature, suffered fatal wounds as well, covered with gashes on his head and upper body. John Doyle and his mother, Mahala, as well as other witnesses, identified John Brown as the ringleader and branded him an assassin.

The news was first reported in the *Westport (Mo.) Border Times* on May 27, alleging there were eight (rather than five) men murdered. The language of the *Saint Louis Morning Herald* reflected popular

sentiment: "midnight assassination which revives in all their atroc-
ity the most fiendish barbarities of the darkest ages and which, we
repeat is without parallel in Christendom since the Revolution in
France, is *deliberately* planned to strike terror into the hearts of political opponents! Whether such will be the effect of the lesson remains to be seen."[28] Antislavery advocates had little to counter
these diatribes.

While the *New York Times* put the story of the Sack of Lawrence
on the front page, it included only a few lines about the Pottawatomie massacre on the inside pages with a disclaimer that the
report was from an unreliable source. At the same time the *New York
Tribune* ran a story that fictionalized the attack, embellishing the incident with hangings, prayers, and dramatic rescues. John Brown's
role in the incident was not reported outside of Kansas. Perhaps
abolitionists did not want it revealed that the Brown family and
Sherman's brother were involved in a lawsuit, a feud that could
have tarnished the purity of Brown's abolitionist motives.

Southern statesmen did not exploit the opportunity to contrast
these midnight murders with Sumner's beating. It was ironically
a crime that both sides wished to bury. The Free-Soilers hoped to
preserve their pristine image, and the proslavery advocates used
the murders as the pretext for their next assault: the Battle of
Osawatomie in August. Hundreds of proslavery men swept into
Brown's Station. One of Brown's sons was killed, and, after this
blow, Brown, a fugitive from a local warrant, fled the territory to return to the East.

The political repercussions of this incident did not emerge until
after Brown's infamy following Harpers Ferry. But the southern
consensus viewed Brown's bloodthirsty side as an outgrowth of his
Kansas rampage—as if he got a "taste" of blood at Osawatomie and
was reduced to a vampirish prowl thereafter. Stealth rather than
brutality determined the weapons at Pottawatomie: Brown's party
wished to avoid gunfire to alarm subsequent victims. But sinister
imagery clearly played on other themes. Accounts emphasized the
helplessness and purity of the slain proslavery men, painted as submissive, even sacrificial, lambs to Brown's "terrible swift sword."

28. Abels, *Man on Fire*, 65–66.

The machete-wielding Osawatomie assassin was a prequel to Harpers Ferry, a story concocted after his sensationalized trial to explain previous events.

The sectional strife revolving around John Brown was a dramatic and important linchpin. The response to his Maryland raid exemplifies sectional conflict's gendered rhetoric. Indeed, Brown's act was the apocalyptic nightmare that awakened proslavery hysterics from their deepest sleeps. Southern sexual politics dictated the stockpiling of venom for Yankee *women* reformers, whom they perceived as the unnatural, Medusa-like monsters emerging from the anthills of the North. They raged against the despised Grimké sisters, Angelina and Sarah, who betrayed their Carolina birth, who penned incendiary tracts, and the younger, nicknamed "Devilina" by southern detractors, even lectured to promiscuous audiences. These figures were the most frightening apparitions in the sectional horror show: plantation bred but breathing the fire and brimstone of antislavery. The Grimkés were the monsters southerners feared most, until eventually an even more phantasmagorical image of evil incarnate appeared—in the guise of John Brown.

At the time and in subsequent historical readings Brown's military operation at Harpers Ferry has been described in sexualized language.[29] Brown's raid is very often referred to in texts as "an attack," as savage, brutish—in short, a figurative "rape." Brown's violation feminized the South and underscored sectional vulnerability. John Brown signaled that campaigns against the slave power could be armed and dangerous. He and his followers were willing to assert their manhood, shed blood for antislavery, and even die for their cause. The passive martyrdom of Elijah Lovejoy, a victim of the mob, was replaced with the vision of John Brown's militancy.[30]

Brown's courage and clarity of purpose created a symbol that

29. This section builds on the work of Bertram Wyatt-Brown ("'A Volcano Beneath a Mountain of Snow': John Brown and the Problem of Interpretation"), Robert McGlone ("John Brown, Henry Wise, and the Politics of Insanity"), and Paul Finkelman ("John Brown and His Raid" and "Manufacturing Martyrdom: The Antislavery Response to John Brown's Raid"), in *His Soul Goes Marching On: Responses to John Brown and the Harpers Ferry Raid,* ed. Paul Finkelman (Charlottesville: University Press of Virginia, 1995).

30. McGlone has carefully chronicled Brown's heroic aspects. See also "Rescripting a Troubled Past: John Brown's Family and the Harpers Ferry Conspiracy," *Journal of American History* 75 (March 1989): 1179–1200.

haunted both North and South. Certainly, abolitionists could and did champion his moral vision. Southerners, in defense, branded Brown as "insane." His dreams of slave insurrections fed into the daily paranoia that kept planters looking over their shoulders.

Even though most northern antislavery leaders repudiated Brown's violence, he was a cause célèbre. His hasty conviction and rapid execution elevated antislavery terrorism into martyrdom. Frederick Douglass argued that Brown "imitated the heroes of Lexington, Concord and Bunker Hill." White abolitionists squabbled over control of Brown's image. Paul Finkelman discovered northern propagandists even wanted to exploit Brown's corpse by trying to wrestle it away from the family to use in a multicity tour to drum up antislavery support.[31]

This protracted struggle over John Brown's legacy had gendered consequences. Male antislavery leadership saw this as an opportunity to break free of the feminization of abolitionism. When L. Maria Child wanted to do a biography of Brown, the project was expropriated by James Redpath. When Child traveled to Virginia to visit Brown in prison, his lawyer turned her away, explaining that we "don't want women there to unman his heroic determination to maintain a firm and consistent composure."[32]

Douglass further harangued, "It is an effeminate and cowardly age which calls a man a lunatic because he rises to such self-forgetful heroism, as to count his own life worth nothing in comparison with the freedom of millions of his fellows."[33] Male abolitionists, and especially many black antislavery activists, welcomed a shift from the age of sentimentality. With the dawning of an era of martial virtue, men were drawn into the cult of true manhood—most vividly through armed aggression and finally war. Indeed, this "ascent to manhood" was a key feature of the black male experience, as W. E. B. Dubois commented: "How extraordinary, and what a tribute to ignorance and religious hypocrisy, is the fact that in the minds of most people, even those of liberals, only murder makes men. The slave pleaded, he was humble; he protected the women of

31. See Finkelman, "Manufacturing Martyrdom," in *His Soul Goes Marching On*, 60.

32. Ibid., 54.

33. Ibid., 60.

the South, and the world ignored him. The slave killed white men; and behold, he was a man."[34]

When Brown and his band of eighteen men, which included armed ex-slaves, seized a federal arsenal in Maryland, they sent shock waves through southern political circles. Craig Simpson has shown in his biography of the Virginia governor that even though Henry Wise condemned Brown to death, he harbored admiration for Brown's manliness. Ralph Waldo Emerson elaborated, "Indeed, it is the *reductio ad absurdum* of slavery, when the Governor of Virginia is forced to hang a man whom he declares to be a man of the most integrity, truthfulness and courage he has ever met."[35]

Brown was viewed as the monstrosity who embodied southerners' worst nightmares. Drenched in blood, armed abolitionists extended their grasp toward southern white males' most precious assets: southern honor and the slave power. With their jewels at risk, the "plantocracy" panicked. An abolitionist willing to die for his principles was one thing but to kill for antislavery was quite another development: an advent too ghastly to contemplate.

Brown's transformation into a charismatic martyr of enormous influence galvanized the slave power. Even as he exhorted his wife in a last letter to his family to "kiss the children," and even as the controversy swirled around his last walk to the gallows—did he kiss a slave child or not?—Brown's image was being creatively cultivated. Brown was sentimentalized on the one hand and brandished like a cudgel in the other: southerners felt clobbered in either case. Brown's legacy provoked extreme ambivalence; Virginian Edmund Ruffin acknowledged Brown's possession of that quality "more highly esteemed by the world than the most rare and perfect virtues . . . physical or animal courage, the most complete fearlessness of and insensibility to danger and death."[36] Not in spite of but because of white southern admiration, Brown had to be put to

34. See Jim Cullen, "'I'se a Man Now': Gender and African-American Men," in *Divided Houses*, 90–91.
35. Craig Simpson, *A Good Southerner: The Life of Henry A. Wise of Virginia* (Chapel Hill: University of North Carolina Press, 1985) (see chapter 11, "Two Men at Harpers Ferry"); Thomas R. Dew, ed., *The John Brown Invasion* (Boston: James Campbell, 1860), 104.
36. William K. Scarborough, ed., *The Diary of Edmund Ruffin* (Baton Rouge: Louisiana State University Press, 1972), 171.

death: he had challenged the slave owners on their own terms. He had trespassed on their own ground, and struck too deep. This violation had explicitly sexual overtones, and African Americans in Baltimore celebrated by scribbling obscene graffiti on a dance floor that depicted Brown's rape of the South.[37]

Even more perversely, Brown was not just an abolitionist fanatic, but an image reflected in a cracked mirror. Brown had not merely hit a nerve but had stripped bare the soul of southern temperament with his daring exploits. Slave owners stared at this impassioned, extremist warrior and saw a glimpse of themselves. It was this fearful recognition, shattered symmetry, that demanded Brown's swift execution.

Brown's legacy foreshadowed the brothers' war. Abolitionists could no longer be trusted to remain nurturing, warm, quasi-feminine. Instead of condemning the Constitution, they might run for office and put an antislavery man in the White House. Abolitionist L. Maria Child, a paragon of feminine influence, was supplanted. Male leadership in the North and the South calibrated their opposition to one another, while women, shunted aside, shuddered in anticipation. After Brown replaced Lovejoy, the tilt toward machismo raised the stakes. Contests over loyalty and blood, legacy and virtue, slavery and honor could no longer be settled by words alone. Men demanded satisfaction, and bullets and battles would follow. Blood would spill, not just on the Senate floor at high noon or a Kansas creek bed at midnight, but until half a million perished.

37. See William McFeely's "Impotent and Static with Rage," lecture delivered at Gettysburg College, July 1992. McFeely's essay deals with Frederick Douglass and John Brown. McFeely surmises that both the South and the North were portrayed as men in this graffiti.

Clio's Daughters

Whence and Whither

VIRGINIA VAN DER VEER HAMILTON

November 1991
Fort Worth, Texas

Marlene [Rikard] asked me about five months ago to make this talk, although she knew that, for personal reasons, I had done no recent research and had no scholarly findings to report. At first I demurred. Then it dawned on me that Marlene might have another type of talk in mind—a talk by a living, breathing artifact: a septuagenarian who received her Ph.D. in the dark ages of 1968—something from personal experience about pioneer days for women in our profession.

Marlene wanted a title immediately because the program was going to press. So I came up with what I considered a catchy title long before putting together any thoughts on the subject.

Fortuitously, the god of our profession is female. And fortunately, we have not had to shed from our professional label a bunch of *es* and *ss*, as have actresses, sculptresses, poetesses, stewardesses, and waitresses. Those were traditional feminine pursuits. Perhaps there were not enough women historians extant to bother inventing the term *historianness*; thus, we have been historians all along.

But, not having *es* and *ss* attached to our professional label is about the only aspect of women in our profession that has escaped prejudice based on gender.

I did do a bit of research for this talk, although I do not offer what I am about to say as definitive or in-depth.

64

What follows may well tend toward the polemic; the older I get, the more polemical. Maybe this is part of the aging process; maybe it stems from the surfacing of ancient grievances.

One other thing I have discovered: nothing loosens the tongue like retirement.

First, I went to my personal library. My glance fell immediately on three books purchased by my parents in 1927 and 1939: *The Rise of American Civilization,* by Charles and Mary Beard. I do not remember that, as a teenager, I took any special interest in this husband-wife combination. We who came of age in the thirties were accustomed to famous twosomes; Eleanor and Franklin, Charles and Anne Lindbergh, Fred Astaire and Ginger Rogers, Edward VIII and Wally.

For insight into the life and thoughts of Mary Ritter Beard, I am indebted to Nancy Cott's new book, *A Woman Making History.* Mary Ritter, born in Indiana in 1876, earned no degree beyond the bachelor of philosophy at DePauw University. She scorned home economics, then considered the proper course of study for women. Years later, DePauw awarded Mary a Phi Beta Kappa key; her grades had merited this honor when Mary was a student, but in the 1870s women were not admitted to Phi Beta Kappa.

Both Beards took it for granted that it was Mary's task to rear their daughter and son. Charles wrote a woman friend: "I know how you feel about the restrictions of young motherhood as well as any mere man can know for Mrs. Beard had everything fall on her young shoulders simultaneously. But in spite of all its limitations, I find her believing that one must somehow work from the family out to public activity."

Mary never signed herself "Mrs. Charles Beard." Still, Cott believes she suffered from lifelong ambivalence about her role; her husband's achievements, his Ph.D., his teaching post at Columbia, and his elections as president of the American Political Science Association and the American Historical Association magnified Mary's insecurity.

To Charles's credit, he insisted that his publisher give full credit to his coauthor. He avoided quoting reviews that singled him out as author, because these were not "true to fact or just to my coworker." Indeed, Cott believes *The Rise of American Civilization* owes much to Mary Beard's integrative concept of history to include cultural as well as political and economic themes. Probably, Charles also owed Mary for the concept of *civilization*—moving toward individual and social progress—as being inherent in history and for her strongly held conviction that women were central to the making of civilization.

Mary received inadequate recognition for her contribution to their jointly written books. *Current Biography* for 1941, under the names Charles Beard and Mary Beard, sketched his life only. One reviewer called a work of the Beards' inferior to a book by Morrison and Commager: "naturally, because in the Beard case, only one scholar has worked on the book." At Charles's death in 1948, his obituaries omitted Mary altogether, referring to *The Rise of American Civilization* as "his" masterpiece, "his" greatest work.

To use Cott's term, Mary "rowed against the intellectual stream," thus provoking organized feminists. Following the suffragist movement, she joined no women's organizations. She profoundly believed that women's rights advocates had misrepresented the past by emphasizing women's domination by men. In her 1946 book, *Woman as Force in History,* Mary argued that the "dogma of women's complete historic subjection to man must be rated as one of the most fantastic myths ever created by the human mind."

The tone of that book reflected Mary's wartime bitterness over the fact that women were collaborating with men in making war; their choice to follow the male model wrecked her whole thesis of women's civilizing presence. Cott categorizes as antifeminist in its thesis the feminist tradition that ever since the eighteenth century had grossly misled women by inducing them to follow the male model instead of their own destinies. Mary Beard, in Cott's view, minimized and distorted the tradition of feminist protest by presenting women as having had a vital shared history at the center, a myth as exaggerated as what Mary Beard considered the myth of women's subjection.

Mary Beard's major task, as Cott sees it, was to insist upon including women in history, both as cooperators with men and as makers of civilization. Her chief contribution was her creativity in women's history. She led the way in founding what was to become a World Center for Women's Archives. She insisted that history looks different through women's eyes and that women have been

central to history making. She expressed her conviction that women
need their history in order to change their future.

On my shelves I found historical works by other women born
during the late nineteenth and early twentieth centuries. Like Beard,
these women married and bore children. Like Beard, none held the
Ph.D. Like Beard, judging by their wide readership and awards,
they became highly successful at writing history.

Esther Forbes, born in Massachusetts in 1891, won the 1942
Pulitzer Prize for *Paul Revere and the World He Lived In* and the New-
berry Medal for *Johnny Tremain.* Forbes's books were translated into
at least ten languages.

Catherine Drinker Bowen, born in Haverford, Pennsylvania, in
1897, won the National Book Award in nonfiction in 1958 for *The
Lion and the Throne: The Life and Times of Sir Edward Coke.* Bowen's
biographies of Tchaikovsky, Oliver Wendell Holmes, and John
Adams and her study of the Constitutional Convention, *Miracle at
Philadelphia,* were all Book of the Month selections in an era when
the Book of the Month signified quality, not simply mass sales.

Barbara Tuchman, born in New York City in 1912, won Pulitzer
Prizes for *The Guns of August* and *Stilwell and the American Experience
in China,* as well as the gold medal for history from the American
Academy of Arts and Sciences. In 1979 Tuchman became the first
woman selected for the National Endowment for the Humanities'
Jefferson Lectureship.

Yet, critics frequently disparaged the books these women wrote.
In 1944, Henry Steele Commager deemed Bowen's *Yankee from
Olympus* "a beautiful piece of workmanship." But the eminent liter-
ary critic Edmund Wilson wrote, "Mrs. Bowen's own mind is too
blunt, too limited, and too prosaic for her to be able to deal with the
Holmses. . . ."

Male condescension had its effect on Bowen. "I'm always *terrified*
of what the scholars are going to say," she told an interviewer. "I'm
not a scholar at all, you know. I've really no business messing
around with this stuff."

Tuchman, too, received her share of negative reviews, particularly
from academicians. Unlike Bowen, Tuchman remained unapolo-
getic. She took pride in being a good storyteller and characterized

herself as a "writer whose subject is history." She took on the professional guild with spirit and guts. "Historians who put in everything plus countless footnotes aren't thinking of their readers," Tuchman said. "Subsequently they're not readable. I never took a Ph.D. It's what saved me, I think. If I had taken a doctoral degree it would have stifled any writing capacity."

Incidentally, I noticed that these women relied on other women for research assistance. Esther Forbes acknowledged her mother as chief collaborator and researcher on *Paul Revere*. Catherine Drinker Bowen dedicated *John Adams and the American Revolution* to a woman friend "whose eye with a manuscript is caustic and skillful and whose friendship has survived good chapters and bad." Barbara Tuchman thanked her daughter, Alma, for "substantial research" on *A Distant Mirror*. Mary Beard, of course, had Charles.

Let's move on to a much larger nonprofessional category of women in history. I am sure all of you are familiar with the academic wife as typist: not only wives who typed book manuscripts but also those—perhaps thousands—who typed their husbands' dissertations. I am hazarding a guess that the era of the wife typist probably began with the invention of the typewriter and dwindled to an end around the late 1970s.

If you take it for granted that the word processor produces words and erases paragraphs with a touch as light as a feather and rearranges pages at the press of a button, you probably never knew what it was like to produce a perfect manuscript of three to four hundred pages on a *manual* (not even electric) typewriter; the toll exacted upon the typist such as broken fingernails, inky smudges on the hands from changing ribbons and carbons, weary shoulders, aching back, spreading rump, and, above all, nervous tension caused by fear that, as one approached the end of a perfect page, a finger might slip, an error result, the entire page to be typed again.

Furthermore, this was no one-time task; husband, critics, and editors almost always required revisions. To produce a three- to four-hundred-page manuscript, a wife might easily type fifteen hundred to two thousand pages. C. Vann Woodward was not exaggerating in 1938 when he expressed appreciation, in the preface to *Tom Watson, Agrarian Rebel*, to "my wife, upon whose shoulders fell the *heavy burden* of typing this manuscript. . . ."

As I browsed among prefaces, I discovered wives who contributed to their husbands' scholarly reputations in ways considerably more sophisticated than typing.

As joint author: In 1922 T. P. Abernathy, who wrote *The South in the New Nation*, said: "my wife . . . *should* have been credited with joint authorship of this book, for she collaborated in all stages of its preparation and contributed an equal share to its production. Unfortunately, there are technical reasons why her name could not appear in the title page, and I hope that I may be absolved of the charge of ingratitude. . . ."

As motivator: In 1929 U. B. Phillips, author of *Life and Labor in the Old South*, wrote: "my wife impelled the beginning of this book. . . ."

As proofreader: In 1934 A. B. Moore, writer of *History of Alabama*, contended: "my wife read critically both the galley and page proofs."

As illustrator: In 1957 John Richard Alden, author of *The South in the Revolution*, acknowledged: "my wife . . . drew the maps for this book."

As researcher: In 1967 George Tindall, who wrote *Emergence of the New South*, described his wife as "my favorite research assistant and critic. . . ."

As ghost writer: In 1970 Paul Gaston, author of *The New South Creed*, said: "my wife types badly and her spelling, punctuation, and proofreading are unreliable, but she persuaded me to pursue the subject in the first place, let few of my paragraphs escape revision, and wrote the passages I like most."

As multifaceted wife: In 1971 Monroe Lee Billington, writer of *The American South*, wrote: "my wife, who served as typist, grammarian, critic, sounding board, and sentry at the study door. . . ."

As understanding wife: In 1974 Alan Barth, author of *Prophets with Honor: Great Dissents and Great Dissenters in the Supreme Court*, admitted: "My wife's help in typing, reading, and talking about the book runs beyond the reach of public acknowledgment. Happily, she understands my gratitude."

And as superwife: In 1956 James McGregor Burns, who wrote *Roosevelt: The Lion and the Fox*, said: "my wife, who (undertook a great deal of research with me . . . helped shape many of the ideas in this volume, and gave the various drafts searching criticism) . . . also managed to perform clerical and stenographic chores and, with the help of the children, to create at home those conditions in which hard and sustained work is possible. . . ."

Wives as typists contributed not only a labor of love but also a labor of necessity, given the paltry level of most academic salaries during the Great Depression. Like sharecroppers, wives performed hard physical labor on someone else's property. Now I grant that many typist wives eventually shared in the profits of their labor: welcome additional income when the dissertation led to tenure and promotion or if the book became a classic and royalty checks arrived in the mail. But I am also painfully aware that a number of wife typists—their bodies no longer supple and their typing skills no longer needed—eventually found themselves, like aging sharecroppers, booted off the property.

The era of academic wives as unpaid helpmates came to a close due to wider career opportunities for married women, more comfortable salaries in academe, heightened sensitivity by husbands, and the word processor.

I checked prefaces by a few younger male scholars. References to wives had moved from the practical to the poetic.

In 1987 Simon Schama, author of *An Embarrassment of Riches*, acknowledged: "the joy of my own family history throughout this project is altogether the creation of my beloved wife. Even a big book seems paltry offering for the daily riches of her companionship."

In 1991 Robert E. Shalhope, who wrote *The Roots of Democracy*, said: "I am grateful to [my wife] for reading the manuscript and sharing her thoughts with me on long walks during a beautiful autumn on the Vineyard. Most of all I am thankful for her abiding love."

Such sentiments have a charming ring, but, in my increasingly choleric frame of mind, I find myself actually preferring this 1990 tribute by the novelist Nicholas Feeling: "My own wife does nothing like other people, and quarreled with me during every day of the writing. When it was finished, she refused point blank to read the book. But since she has been the beat of my heart for thirty-seven years, I must add: 'To Renee.' "

When I was a college student in the thirties and forties, women teachers were conditioned to believe that high school was their proper and ultimate sphere. Well into the seventies, women continued to encounter the high school syndrome. A woman about fifteen or twenty years younger than I recently confided this experience: when she started to fill out her applications for admission to the history graduate program at a southern university, she was advised by a male friend: "When you get to the part where they ask you to check your goal, be sure to check high school teaching. They won't accept you if you check Ph.D. They don't believe women have any business teaching at the college level."

My friend checked high school teaching, eventually earned her Ph.D., became a respected and popular teacher, published widely, and received a number of major grants. She is now a tenured full professor, but the fact that, years later, she still does not feel comfortable about having this small incident publicly attributed to her says something about continuing apprehension of male hostility.

Now let's take a brief look at *fully* qualified professional women historians prior to World War II. Dr. Lucille Griffith remembers the faculty of Alabama College for Women, now the University of Montevallo, in the late thirties and forties as having been about 75 percent women, most of them single, and many holding degrees from prestigious eastern or middle-western universities. The 1941 catalog of Alabama College verifies Griffith's recollection: its faculty and administration consisted of ninety-one females, twenty-four males, including the president, dean, and business manager. Ten women held Ph.D.s earned during the twenties and thirties at Stanford, Cornell, two at Chicago, Yale, Iowa, Duke, Wisconsin, North Carolina, and Peabody. "These women were good teachers who couldn't get jobs elsewhere," Griffith recalled. "When members of Dr. Hallie Farmer's family first came to visit her in Montevallo in 1927, they were horrified at the sight of this tiny, dusty, remote Alabama town and begged Hallie to come back to the Midwest."

Hallie Farmer, who earned a Ph.D. in history at the University of Wisconsin, made a virtue of necessity. She spent her entire thirty-year career at Alabama College, becoming without doubt the strongest member of its faculty, radiating energy and vigor in her trademark somber black dresses, her advice heeded even by male deans and presidents.

From the unlikely base of a small sheltered women's college, Farmer became a statewide leader for reforms. She was instrumental in placing women on juries, abolition of the poll tax, ending the arbitrary reading tests administered to would-be voters by boards of registrar, banning the whipping of state prisoners, and establishing a School for Citizenship at her college to instruct women students how laws were passed and to encourage them to take part in this process.

In the late 1950s, after Farmer had led that faculty for more than twenty years, serving under a series of male presidents, she was finally offered the presidency of this women's college. "It's too late," said Farmer. "I don't have the strength for that job now."

In search of experiences of women seeking to enter the field of history at the college level after World War II, I interviewed six retired historians, myself included. Here are some of our recollections.

On attending graduate school in the fifties: Lucille Griffith, although she held an M.A. from Tulane, received this unsolicited advice from the head of the Duke history department when he rejected her application: "Don't do it . . . it's too hard on a woman's nervous system, they can't take the pressure." Although the reason was not so graphically spelled out, Griffith was also rejected by Vanderbilt, North Carolina, Texas, and Rochester.

When she applied to Brown, Griffith was informed by the historian Barney Keeney, dean of the graduate school, that his university "didn't usually take women of her age." (Griffith was in her mid-forties because she had been teaching high school, at a junior college, and with a master's degree at Alabama College for Women.) Normally mild-mannered, Griffith wrote Keeney what she later remembered as a "sassy letter," insisting she had a reputation of finishing what she started. Evidently, her letter burned itself into Keeney's memory. "Oh yes," he told a mutual acquaintance years later, "she's the one who wrote me *that* letter." Probably due to *that* letter, Griffith was accepted.

Candidates who failed their orals at Brown in those days were allowed to try again; around 50 percent of males, as Griffith remembers, availed themselves of this second chance. But Griffith passed her colonial and early American fields on the first try. Her examiners told her that—nervous system notwithstanding—she had been the best-prepared candidate who had presented herself to them in the past eight years.

Ph.D. in hand in 1957, Griffith returned to her position as assistant professor at Alabama College for Women; Keeney became president of Brown.

Frances Roberts, trying to be the best-possible high school teacher, studied for two summers under Frank Owsley at Vanderbilt. When Owsley moved to Tuscaloosa after World War II, Roberts finished a master's degree there and eased, without anybody taking much notice of it, onto the Ph.D. track.

However, she soon encountered John Ramsay, a leading Europeanist, with the then widespread male notion that the Ph.D. was wasted on women: being destined to marry and keep house, they probably would never use their degrees. Ramsay's highly regarded "Age of Reason" course attracted a large undergraduate and graduate enrollment. Not knowing his students by name, he graded solely on the basis of written papers. Roberts signed her papers simply "F. Roberts." During her first six hours in his courses, she received As on all papers and an A in Ramsay's course. But eventually Ramsay discovered that "F. Roberts" was "Frances Roberts" (with an *e*). Her grades in his courses immediately dropped to Bs, and there they remained.

In 1956 Frances Roberts became the first woman to receive a Ph.D. in history from the University of Alabama.

Although Roberts breached the sex barrier, no other females enrolled in the history doctoral program at Tuscaloosa for almost a decade. I was one of two who did. Most members of the all-male history faculty regarded *me* with incredulity: where had *this* woman come from: married, a mother, and in her mid-forties, who did not plan to pay homage in the role of a teaching assistant, but held a full-time job in Birmingham and commuted to campus.

One of my professors, James F. Doster, at the start of each seminar, never failed to explain my presence to his male students thus: "Mrs. Hamilton is" (as if revealing a former profession only slightly more respectable than prostitution) "a journalist." (And, judging by his tone of voice, likely to remain one.)

Eventually, it became this man's lot to direct my dissertation. I had suggested the topic of the Scottsboro trials, not yet the topic of a scholarly book. Deep frown. "No, no, no, Mrs. Hamilton. That is a dirty case. I cannot have you working on it."

Long before I reached the dissertation stage, the acknowledged leader of the Americanists at Tuscaloosa, Thomas B. Alexander, took it upon himself to assure me solemnly at least once, often twice, every semester: "Mrs. Hamilton, you cannot *possibly* do it!" Those words, delivered with such assurance, burned themselves into my nervous system.

I must testify, however, that by the mid-sixties, John Ramsay had experienced a change of heart. After reading my first seminar paper, he told me: "Mrs. Hamilton, it would be a shame if you did not go ahead and finish." Those few words may well have saved me from giving up.

As a form of academic penance, I was required to spend a semester technically "in residence." I lived in the graduate women's dormitory. Male students called this the "lesbian hall."

Eventually, I passed my orals. The "you cannot *possibly* do it" faculty member had been one of my examiners. He was, shall we say, "man enough" to declare: "Well, if I had a hat, I'd eat it." If only I had worn a hat!

Twelve years after Roberts, Marjorie Howell Cook and I became the second and third females to receive history doctorates at Tuscaloosa.

The man who tried so hard to discourage me left for another university and became president of the SHA. In later years, I was always amazed to observe him vigorously pursuing various young women with offers of jobs in his department.

Mildred Caudle followed Roberts, Cook, and me on the doctoral track at Tuscaloosa. She met with no overt references to her sex unless such was implicit in the chairman's stern warning that her quest would be "excruciatingly difficult." The effect of these words was to make Caudle even more determined; her work—like Griffith's performance on her orals—must be not of mere passing quality, but the absolute best.

She took her initial course from John Ramsay. Following the first test, he dressed down his class for their inadequate performances, and then picked up one paper to read aloud: "Now *that's* what I wanted," he told the class. It was Caudle's paper.

Do not suppose, however, that grade discrimination based on sex has ended. One of my former all-A students who entered the Ph.D. program in the 1980s told me this incident. Shocked to receive a B from one of our widely known colleagues, she asked him to point out her problem. Her response to his question, he informed her, had been "typically female."

I inquired how women doctoral candidates got along with the male fellow students who flooded campuses after World War II.

Camaraderie did develop. Nonetheless, some women felt obliged to defer to male peers. In the mid-1950s, Wynss Shepard remembers, she voluntarily withdrew her name from the list of candidates for officers in the Graduate History Club at the University of Pennsylvania. "I just believed," she told me, "that the main offices belong to men. I thought women were only supposed to serve as 'secretary.' "

Shepard remembers that, like male professors, male students found it hard to take female colleagues seriously. They, too, were convinced that women would eventually marry and assume traditional pursuits. Shepard also recalls an undercurrent of rivalry: "What if this woman should get my job?"

Shepard married and took the then traditional path, thinking, "Someone has to be with the children." Neither she nor her husband, an M.D., ever entertained the possibility that *he* would assume this role. All her life, Shepard, a Fulbright in France on her record and her Ph.D. from Penn on the wall, voluntarily limited her career to part-time teaching.

Female Ph.Ds. in history, who had the misfortune to marry men in the same discipline, found themselves taking the backseat. At Penn, Shepard had the then unusual experience of being taught by two women, both of whom held Ph.D. degrees. These women were classified as "associates": marriage to male historians barred them, by university rules, from permanent faculty status.

Roberts remembers a three-hour argument with the president of the Huntsville campus of the University of Alabama over whether a highly qualified woman Ph.D. should be allowed to teach in the history department of which her husband was a member. The president gave the widely used excuse: nepotism. In this case, Roberts eventually prevailed, but for years this woman, Roberts recalled, "had, up to a point, to stay in the background."

Some things do change. Roberts told me with a chuckle of a recent case in which a man was hired as *president* so the university could attract to its faculty a renowned physicist—his *wife*.

On serving as department head: The feeling—whether accurate or not—that first-class male scholars could not be recruited by a female department head was widespread in the late sixties and early seventies. I had a chance to assume the UAB history chairmanship in that era but accepted the folk wisdom that I simply would not be able to recruit qualified males. It was 1975 before I put this timidity behind me and took on the chair of my department.

As chair at Huntsville, Roberts, on the advice of her all-male faculty and perhaps remembering her graduate school experience, signed all recruitment correspondence "F. Roberts."

Lucille Griffith finally achieved the headship of her department after having been twice passed over for males, one young enough to have been her son. When she set in to recruit, Griffith felt obliged to ask male candidates if they minded working under a woman. During the seventies, teaching positions were hard to come by. Most males swore to Griffith that gender mattered not in the least. But one, perhaps more candid, hesitated, then responded: "Well, I guess it wouldn't matter. After all, I've worked for a lot of second-class men." He did *not* get the job.

Adding a second woman to a history faculty was often a slow process and one that *had* to be led by the original woman member, the prevalent male attitude having been "we already *have* a woman in our department."

Unfortunately, some senior women felt comfortable with the status of token female—indeed, even felt threatened by the possibility of a second woman in their domain. They cloaked such feelings in expressions such as, "The matter of gender just didn't come up. We were looking for the most highly qualified person." As we all know, "most highly qualified" is almost always a judgment call.

In the early years of affirmative action, I set out to add a second female to the UAB history department. I had gotten into that department because I was the second person hired to teach history at UAB as it moved from extension to full university status; in other words, I got there ahead of all but one male, and—no one else wanting or qualified to do the office routine—I moved up to chair.

In this case, we had to choose which of two finalists was more "highly qualified," a male or a female. On voting day, I caught the department by surprise by temporarily relinquishing the chair to a male colleague and offering a motion that—all other qualifications being roughly equal—the principle of affirmative action should be controlling. What a brouhaha: to this day, I remember who voted for and who voted against my motion. The female, Harriet Amos Doss, got the job. Thereafter, the matter of a candidate's sex became, I am glad to say, almost immaterial; the department today is about evenly divided as to gender.

I have no expertise whatever on the experience of women historians in large and prestigious eastern universities. But about twelve years ago I did have one dispiriting glimpse into that world. A renowned historian, C. Vann Woodward, came to lecture on the UAB campus. I had admired his writings and learned from them, so I jumped at the chance to take him to dinner before his lecture. Over dinner, I inquired as to the size of his department. Well over one hundred, he guessed. How many were women? I asked innocently. This man had written eloquently about the disadvantaged and powerless in the South. He had been one of those prominent historians who had marched at Selma. But he appeared to be massively indifferent to the matter of women in our profession: "Maybe three or four," he told me. "I really don't know," or care, I took it. Following his lecture, he departed in a crowd of male "groupies," not bothering to thank me for dinner.

Now the widespread, ultimate, and perhaps ongoing discriminatory weapon: women's salaries compared to those of men.

At one point in her student career, Shepard applied to the employment office at Penn. "Well," a man informed her, "this job is supposed to pay seven thousand, but, since you are a woman, you might get six."

Evelyn Wiley, who recollected no sex discrimination during her years as a graduate student at Penn (on a fellowship reserved for women) and no problems with her all-male colleagues in the history department at Birmingham-Southern College, did remember that her salary was less than that of comparable males. In the days of deep secrecy over the matter of salaries, Wiley discovered this by simply asking a male colleague. "But I didn't make any 'to-do' over it," she recalled. "No lawsuit or anything like that. I just accepted it."

When Athens College became a state institution in the 1970s and salaries a matter of public record, Caudle learned for the first time that, although a Ph.D., she was being paid below most men, including some with *master's* degrees. Infuriated, she confronted the president. His explanation came readily: "These men have families to support," the inference being that Caudle, being married, did not need a salary comparable to that of a man.

Roberts had earned her doctorate and taught for eleven years at the Huntsville campus of the University of Alabama, when she discovered—in the course of her extra duty of keeping the college's financial records—that a *new instructor* in engineering had just been offered ten thousand dollars at a time when her salary was sixty-five hundred. Roberts summoned up the courage to complain. She was offered a three-hundred-dollar raise, "the best we could do." In Roberts's case, the excuse that she was married did not apply; no one considered the fact that she was the major supporter of an aged aunt, which made her a head of household. She took her case to the president and received some redress in the form of a presidential raise.

Even after Roberts had been on the payroll of the University of Alabama Extension Division for twenty-five years, she still suffered from salary discrimination. She and the only other female full professor, whose field was math, eventually received presidential raises when it became painfully apparent—even to male administrators—that two *women* were the lowest-paid full professors in the entire Extension Division.

I vividly remember my reaction to a similar discovery. Like Wiley, I had "taken it" when I learned from a male friend that I made considerably less than men who held the same jobs in the Washington bureau of the Associated Press. I had taken it, also, when I was told by the business manager at Birmingham-Southern College that, in setting my meager salary, he—like the president of Athens—took into account the fact that I was married and not the sole support of a household. No laws protected Wiley, Roberts, Caudle, and me; we needed our salaries, however skewed, to help feed our families and pay our mortgages.

But by the late 1970s, I had advanced through the ranks at UAB for more than a decade, achieved full-professor status, served as department head, published two books, and had been a member of the faculty longer than all but two others. The then dean of Social and Behavioral Sciences, in a rare moment of candor, released, with no names attached, the salaries of his twelve full professors, all males except me. Going down the list, I finally found my salary: number nine, barely above those males widely and deservedly reputed to be the school's worst teachers and overall do-nothings.

Perhaps tenure emboldened me; undoubtedly, three decades of being valued below men had inflicted deep scars on my self-esteem. Trembling with rage, I confronted the dean, vita in hand. The following week, my salary was "adjusted": number six. But eventually, still the sole female professor, I made it to the top of that salary list.

I have tried to suggest some aspects of "whence." Now I need to refer to "whither," although, I am the first to admit, whither is *your* job, not mine.

One obvious area of "whither" is administration: sexual harassment, as the Anita Hill/Clarence Thomas encounter made clear, is about power. And power, in academe, resides in administration.

My brief survey on this matter is not encouraging. Roberts, Griffith, Wiley, Caudle, and I—all of whom served as chairs of our departments—were succeeded by men. I can report only one bit of encouragement: Roberts's former department today is headed by a woman, Johanna Shields.

Alabama College, while a women's institution, *never* had a woman as president or dean; Judson College, *still* a women's college, has never had a woman president or dean. Athens College, during its era as a women's college, had two women presidents; since it became coeducational, it has been headed by male presidents and deans.

After Alabama College for Women became the University of Montevallo, men began to dominate its faculty. Fifty years after that faculty consisted of roughly 75 percent females, the 1991 catalog shows it to be made up of 110 males and 69 females; 36 of the 110 males (about one-third) are full professors; 15 of the 69 females are, about one-fourth. Only one major administrator—the vice president for student affairs—is female. Five males hold deanships, no females; 9 males chair departments, including the sciences, math, and traffic safety; 5 females chair departments, including art, home economics, and secondary-school administration.

The 1941 history department, headed by Hallie Farmer, had been composed of 4 women and 1 man. The 1991 department is made up of 5 men and 1 woman. Obviously, at this former women's college, the switch to coeducation diminished the status of women on its faculty.

Whither in research? I confess to a kind of Mary Poppins view of this subject. Without doubt, we need authors to rescue women from obscurity. But is it advisable for women to work solely in women's history? Personally—and I have written biographies of two *men*—I hope that women biographers will take *men* as well as women as their subjects, as did Catherine Drinker Bowen and Esther Forbes. After all, a goodly number of men now take *women* as their topics: among the ads in our current program alone, I found books about women written or edited by Melton McLaurin, Charles East, Patrick Geary, Jeffrey Stewart, David C. Smith, and Harold Woodell. C. Vann Woodward won a Pulitzer Prize by editing the diaries of Mary Boykin Chesnut; Darden Asbury Pyron wrote the new biography of Margaret Mitchell. Better watch out: men will take over the most salable women.

I hope women will also follow the leads of Barbara Tuchman and Mary Beard in tackling the big canvas. In the index of her 1978 book about the fourteenth century, Tuchman included the category "women," with such subtitles as mothers, beauty treatment, in courtly love, sexuality, roles in marriage, professors, doctors, in trade, scolds and shrews, and patient Griselda as type.

In the index of *his* major work, *An Embarrassment of Riches: Dutch Culture in the Golden Age,* published ten years later, Simon Schama also included a category for women with subtitles such as cleanliness, in labor force, legal rights of, misogynist satires about, pregnant, and smoking by.

Tuchman's references to women occur on 61 of 597 pages of *A Distant Mirror.* Schama's references to women occur on 66 of 612 pages of *An Embarrassment of Riches.* About 10 percent in both cases, give or take a page. Neither book, incidentally, includes an index category titled "men"; obviously, it was a man's world from the fourteenth through the seventeenth centuries.

Eric Foner's and John Garraty's 1991 encyclopedic *Reader's Companion to American History* also indexes women but not men; the categories women, suffrage, and feminism account for 123 of 1,244 pages. I checked the Foner/Garraty index for entries of individuals. By the time I finished the *es*, I had counted 275 men and 38 women. I quit at this point, having no reason to believe that from *f* to *z* the balance would measurably change. In terms of raising consciousness of women's role in history we are making glacial progress.

In conclusion, although the wife typist, the philosophy of "check high school," the excuse of nepotism, the term *lesbian hall*, and remarks like "after all, I've worked for a lot of second-class men" have, I hope, been consigned to the ash heap of twentieth-century history, two major challenges lie ahead for you who have several more decades in our profession. First, find your way into those traditional preserves of male power: department chairs, deanships, and presidencies. Second, spread the story of women's roles in survey and advanced courses, and on the written record. Accomplish this to such a degree that it will no longer be customary for women to preach, as I assume I have been doing today, largely to the converted.

If you succeed eventually in reaching these goals, the Southern Association for Women Historians can become like the American Woman Suffrage Association, the National Women's Party, the Women's Christian Temperance Union, and Southern Women for the Prevention of Lynching, a dinosaur in an encyclopedia of the past.

Columbus Meets Pocahontas
in the American South

November 1992
Atlanta, Georgia

THEDA PERDUE

As icons of the European colonization of the Americas, Columbus and Pocahontas represent opposite sides of the experience—European and Native, invader and defender, man and woman. Biographies and other scholarly writings document their lives and deeds, but these feats pale in comparison to the encounter these two legendary figures symbolize. Columbus embodies European discovery, invasion, and conquest, while Pocahontas has become the "mother of us all," a nurturing, beckoning, seductive symbol of New World hospitality and opportunity.[1] The two never actually met in the American South, of course, except metaphorically, but this symbolic encounter involved a sexual dynamic that was inherent to the whole process of European colonization, particularly that of the American South.

John Smith's tale of succor and salvation fixed the Pocahontas image forever in the American mind, and his autobiographical account of peaceful relations with her

---

1. Samuel Eliot Morison, *Admiral of the Ocean Sea* (New York: Little, Brown, 1942); Grace Steele Woodward, *Pocahontas* (Norman: University of Oklahoma Press, 1969); J. A. Leo Lemay, *Did Pocahontas Save Captain John Smith?* (Athens: University of Georgia Press, 1993); Philip Young, "The Mother of Us All," *Kenyon Review* 24 (1962): 391–441. See also Rayna Green, "The Pocahontas Perplex: The Image of Indian Women in American Culture," *Massachusetts Review* 16 (1975): 698–714.

people, the Powhatans, has exempted Englishmen from the tarring Columbus has received as an international symbol of aggression. The Columbian encounter with Native women seemed, in fact, to be radically different from Smith's. On his initial voyage of discovery, Columbus had relatively little to report about Native women except that they, like men, went "naked as the day they were born." The loss of one of his ships on this voyage forced Columbus to leave about a third of his crew on Hispaniola. When he returned, he found the burned ruins of his settlement and the decomposing corpses of his men. Local Natives related that "soon after the Admiral's departure those men began to quarrel among themselves, each taking as many women and as much gold as he could." They dispersed throughout the island, and local caciques killed them. The men on Columbus's expedition had their revenge: "Incapable of moderation in their acts of injustice, they carried off the women of the islanders under the very eyes of their brothers and their husbands." Columbus personally presented a young woman to one of his men, Michele de Cuneo, who later wrote that when she resisted him with her fingernails, he "thrashed her well, for which she raised such unheard of screams that you would not have believed your ears." In the accounts of the conquistadores, Spaniards seized women as they seized other spoils of war.[2] Such violence contributed to the "black legend" of Spanish inhumanity to Native peoples and stands in stark contrast to early English descriptions of their encounters with Native women.

John Smith, according to his own account, did not face the kind of resistance from Pocahontas and other Native women of the Virginia tidewater that the Spanish had met in the Caribbean. When Smith and a delegation from Jamestown called at the primary town of Powhatan, Pocahontas's father, they discovered, was away, but the chief's daughter and other women invited the Englishmen to a *mascarado*. "Thirtie young women," Smith wrote, "came naked out of the woods, only covered behind and before with a few green leaves, their bodies all painted." They sang and danced with "infernal

---

2. Marvin Lunenfeld, ed., *1492: Discovery, Invasion, Encounter* (Lexington, Mass.: D. C. Heath, 1991), 133, 161–64; S. E. Morison, ed., *Journals and Other Documents in the Life and Voyages of Christopher Columbus* (New York: Heritage Press, 1963), 212.

passions" and then invited Smith to their lodgings. By his account, written with uncharacteristic modesty in the third person, "he was no sooner in the house, but all these Nymphes more tormented him then ever, with crowding, pressing, and hanging about him, most tediously crying, Love you not me? Love you not me?"[3]

The contrast is obvious: the Spanish supposedly raped and pillaged while the English nobly resisted seduction. By focusing merely on the colonizing Europeans, however, we lose sight of the Native women who are central actors in this drama: they are, after all, both the victims of Columbus's barbarity and the seductive sirens luring Smith's party. Despite differences in the ways these women are portrayed in historical sources, their experiences suggest that conquest and colonization had their own sexual dynamic. One of the facts of colonization that rarely surfaces in polite conversation or scholarly writing is sex, yet we know from the written records left by Europeans and from the more obscure cultural traditions of Native people that European men had sexual relations with Native American women. What can the Columbian voyages, the Jamestown colonists, and the experiences of subsequent European immigrants to the American South tell us about the ways in which men and women crossed cultural and racial bounds in their sexual relations? What do these relationships reveal about European views of female sexuality? And how did these views shape European expansion?

One thing seems fairly certain: Native women were never far from the conscious thought of European men, be they Spanish or English. Nudity ensured that this was so. Accustomed to enveloping clothes, Europeans marveled at the remarkably scant clothing of the Natives. De Cuneo described the Carib woman whom he raped as "naked according to their custom," and Smith noted that except for a few strategically placed leaves, his hostesses were "naked." De Cuneo and Smith were not alone in commenting on Native women's lack of clothing. The Lord Admiral himself noticed not only that the Caribbean women he encountered wore little but also that they had "very pretty bodies." The Jamestown colonists first

---

3. John Smith, *The Generall Historie of Virginia, New England and the Summer Isles* . . . (London, 1624), 3:67.

encountered the prepubescent Pocahontas frolicking naked with the cabin boys. The combination of her youthful enthusiasm as well as her nudity led William Strachey, official chronicler of the colony, to describe Pocahontas as "a well featured, but wanton young girl." Other Europeans also tended to link the absence of clothing to sexuality: Amerigo Vespucci, for whom America was named, noted that "the women . . . go about naked and are very libidinous."[4]

While Native women frequently exposed breasts, particularly in warm weather, they normally kept pudenda covered. When women did bare all, Europeans had another shock in store: Native women in many societies plucked their pubic hair. While some evidence points to female singeing of pubic hair in ancient Greece and even early modern Spain, most Europeans recoiled from hairless female genitalia. Thomas Jefferson, whose interests extended far beyond politics, attempted to explain hair plucking among Native Americans: "With them it is disgraceful to be hairy in the body. They say it likens them to hogs. They therefore pluck the hair as fast as it appears." Jefferson revealed both the reaction of non-Native men and the artificiality of the practice: "The traders who marry their women, and prevail on them to discontinue this practice say, that nature is the same with them as with whites."[5] However comfortable Euro-American men may have been with visible penises, depilation left female genitalia far more exposed than most could bear. Because women revealed their private parts intentionally, they seemed to be flaunting their sexuality.

Another cultural modification to the female physique also provoked comment. Among many Native peoples, women as well as men wore tattoos. While some Euro-Americans became so enamored of the practice that they adopted it, others regarded tattooing in the same light as makeup applied to make one more physically attractive. The late-eighteenth-century Philadelphia physician Benjamin Rush, for example, compared the body markings of Native peoples to cosmetics used by the French, a people whom he

---

4. Woodward, *Pocahontas*, 5; Robert E. Berkhofer, *The White Man's Indian: The History of an Idea from Columbus to the Present* (New York: Alfred A. Knopf, 1978), 7–9.
5. Paul Leicester Ford, ed., *The Writings of Thomas Jefferson* (New York: G. P. Putnam's Sons, 1892–1899), 3:154–55.

described as "strangers to what is called delicacy in the intercourse of the sexes with each other."[6] Unnatural markings on the body, to Europeans, signaled an enhanced sexuality.

As contact between Native peoples and Europeans grew, women gave up tattooing and hair plucking, and they adopted the blouses and long skirts common among non-Native women along the colonial frontier. Other features of Native culture, however, perpetuated the view of Native women as sexually uninhibited. Some Europeans found the humor of Native women to be terribly bawdy. Most women enjoyed teasing and joking, and pranks and jokes with sexual overtones were not necessarily taboo. The teasing Smith endured—"Love you not me? Love you not me?"—is a good example. One Native woman even managed to shock a Frenchman. Louis Philippe made a tour of the American West at the end of the eighteenth century, and during his visit to the Cherokees his guide made sexual advances to several women. "They were so little embarrassed," wrote the future French king, "that one of them who was lying on a bed put her hand on his trousers before my very eyes and said scornfully, *Ah sick.*"[7]

Directness characterized courtship as well as rejection. Smith clearly expressed amazement at the forwardness of the "thirtie young women." In *Notes on the State of Virginia*, Thomas Jefferson compared the "frigidity" of the Native men with the assertiveness of women: "A celebrated warrior is oftener courted by the females, than he has occasion to court: and this is a point of honor which the men aim at. . . . Custom and manners reconcile them to modes of acting, which, judged by Europeans would be deemed inconsistent with the rules of female decorum and propriety."[8] When the epitome of the American Enlightenment attributed Native women with a more active libido than Native men, who could doubt that it was so?

The arrangement and use of domestic space seemed to confirm

6. George W. Corner, ed., *The Autobiography of Benjamin Rush: His Travels through Life, Together with His Commonplace Book [1789–1813]*, Memoirs of the American Philosophical Society (Princeton: Princeton University Press, 1948), 25:71.

7. Louis Philippe, *Diary of My Travels in America*, trans. Stephen Becker (New York: Delacorte Press, 1977), 84–85.

8. Thomas Jefferson, *Notes on Virginia* (1787; reprint, Philadelphia: Matthew Carey, 1794), 299.

a lack of modesty on the part of Native women. Native housing afforded little privacy for bathing, changing what little clothes women did wear, or engaging in sexual intercourse. Several generations, as well as visitors, usually slept in the same lodge. The essayist Samuel Stanhope Smith admitted that Indians were unjustly "represented as licentious because they are seen to lie promiscuously in the same wigwam." Nevertheless, few Natives allowed the lack of privacy in their homes to become a barrier to sexual fulfillment. During early-eighteenth-century explorations in Carolina, one of John Lawson's companions took a Native "wife" for the night, and the newlyweds consummated their "marriage" in the same room in which other members of the expedition feasted and slept: "Our happy Couple went to Bed together before us all and with as little Blushing, as if they had been Man and Wife for 7 Years."[9]

Most European accounts of Native women in the South commented on their sexual freedom, particularly before they married. In the late eighteenth century, naturalist Bernard Romans observed: "Their women are handsome, well made, only wanting the colour and cleanliness of our ladies, to make them appear lovely in every eye; . . . they are lascivious, and have no idea of chastity in a girl, but in married women, incontinence is severely punished; a savage never forgives that crime." John Lawson suggested that even married women "sometimes bestow their Favours also to some or others in their Husbands Absence." And the trader James Adair maintained that "the Cherokees are an exception to all civilized or savage nations in having no law against adultery; they have been a considerable while under a petti-coat government, and allow their women full liberty to plant their brows with horns as oft as they please, without fear of punishment."[10]

Women in the Southeast sometimes openly solicited sex from

9. Samuel Stanhope Smith, *An Essay on the Causes of the Variety of Complexion and Figure in the Human Species*, ed. Winthrop D. Jordan (1810; reprint, Cambridge: Harvard University Press, 1965), 128; John Lawson, *A New Voyage to Carolina*, ed. Hugh T. Lefler (Chapel Hill: University of North Carolina Press, 1967), 37–38.

10. Bernard Romans, *A Concise History of East and West Florida* (1775; reprint, Gainesville: University Press of Florida, 1962), 40–43; Lawson, *New Voyage*, 194; James Adair, *Adair's History of the North American Indians*, ed. Samuel Cole Williams (Johnson City, Tenn.: Watauga Press, 1930), 152–53.

Euro-Americans because sex gave women an opportunity to participate in the emerging market economy. Unlike men, who exchanged deerskins, beaver pelts, and buffalo hides with Europeans for manufactured goods, women often had to rely on "the soft passion" to obtain clothing, kettles, knives, hoes, and trinkets. Among some Native peoples a kind of specialization developed, according to John Lawson, who claimed that coastal Carolina peoples designated "trading girls." Sometimes prostitution was more widespread. Louis Philippe insisted that "all Cherokee women are public women in the full meaning of the phrase: dollars never fail to melt their hearts."[11]

Selling sex was one thing; the apparent gift of women by their husbands and fathers was quite another. To Europeans, sex was a kind of commodity, purchased from prostitutes with money and from respectable women with marriage. An honorable man protected the chastity of his wife and daughters as he would other property. Native men in many societies, however, seemed to condone or even encourage sexual relations between Europeans and women presumably "belonging" to them. Even husbands who might object to "secret infidelities" sometimes offered their wives to visitors.[12]

Europeans also viewed the widespread practice of polygyny, or a man taking more than one wife, as adulterous because they recognized only the first as the "real" wife. Many Native people favored sororal polygyny, the marriage of sisters to the same man, and the groom often took sisters as brides at the same time. Since this meant, in the European terms, that a man married his sister-in-law, sororal polygamy was incest as well as adultery. Jedidiah Morse, in his *Universal Geography*, wrote: "When a man loves his wife, it is considered his duty to marry her sister, if she has one. Incest and bestiality are common among them."[13] Morse apparently regarded marriage to sisters as serious a violation of European sexual mores as human intercourse with animals; in his mind, both constituted perversion.

11. Lawson, *New Voyage*, 41; Louis Philippe, *Diary of My Travels*, 72.
12. Romans, *Concise History*, 40–43.
13. Jedidiah Morse, *The American Universal Geography; or a View of the Present State of All the Kingdoms, States, and Colonies in the Known World* (Thomas and Andrews, 1812), 105.

Polygynous, adulterous, and incestuous or not, marriage meant little to Indians in the estimation of many Euro-Americans. Lawson, for example, described the ease with which the Native peoples of coastal Carolina altered their marital status: "The marriages of these Indians are no further binding than the man and woman agree together. Either of them has the liberty to leave the other upon any frivolous excuse they can make." The trader Alexander Longe relayed a Cherokee priest's view of his people's lax attitude toward marriage: "They had better be asunder than together if they do not love one another but live for strife and confusion."[14] Europeans would have preferred that they stay together and, despite domestic turmoil, raise their children in an appropriately patriarchal household.[15]

When husband and wife parted, children normally remained with their mothers because Native peoples of the Southeast were matrilineal, that is, they traced kinship solely through women. John Lawson attributed this very odd way of reckoning kin, in his view, to "fear of Impostors; the Savages knowing well, how much Frailty possesses *Indian* women, betwixt the Garters and the Girdle." While paternity might be questioned, maternity could not be. Despite the logic of such a system, Europeans had both intellectual and practical objections. Matrilineality seemed too close to the relationship between a cow and calf or a bitch and puppies: it was, the Iroquois historian Cadwallader Colden asserted, "according to the natural course of all animals." "Civilized" man presumably had moved beyond this "natural course" and had adopted laws, civil and religious, that bound fathers to children and husbands to wives. Europeans who married Native women of matrilineal societies nevertheless had difficulty exercising any control over their children and often abandoned them to their mothers' kin because men had no proprietary interest in their offspring. Thomas Nairne wrote of the Creeks: "A Girles Father has not the least hand or concern

14. Lawson, *New Voyage*, 193; Alexander Longe, "A Small Postscript of the Ways and Manners of the Indians Called Charikees," ed. D. H. Corkran, *Southern Indian Studies* 21 (1969): 30.

15. Morse, *American Universal Geography*, 575–76; Albert Gallatin, "Synopsis of the Indian Tribes within the United States East of the Rocky Mountains," vol. 2 of *Archaelogia Americana: Transactions and Collections of American Antiquarian Society* (Worcester, Mass.: Folson, Wells, and Thurston, 1836), 112–13.

in matching her. . . . Sons never enjoy their fathers place and dignity."[16]

Blatant disregard of marital vows and paternal prerogatives was shocking enough, but many Native peoples exhibited little concern for the chastity of their daughters. Jean-Bernard Bossu reported that among Native peoples on the lower Mississippi, "when an unmarried brave passes through a village, he hires a girl for a night or two, as he pleases, and her parents find nothing wrong with this. They are not at all worried about their daughter and explain that her body is hers to do with as she wishes." Furthermore, according to Lawson, "multiplicity of Gallants never [gave] . . . a Stain to a Female's reputation, or the least Hindrance of her Advancement . . . the more *Whorish* the more *Honourable*."[17]

European men who traveled through the Native Southeast thought that they had stepped through the looking glass into a sexual wonderland. Actually, they had encountered only a fractured reflection of their own assumptions about appropriate sexual behavior. Native women were not as uninhibited as most whites thought. Europeans failed to realize that Native peoples did have rules regulating marriage and sexual intercourse, although the rules were sometimes quite different from their own. In the Southeast, unmarried people could engage freely in sex, but many factors other than marital status regulated and limited sexuality. A warrior preparing for or returning from battle (sometimes much of the summer), a ballplayer getting ready for a game, a man on the winter hunt (which could last three to four months), a pregnant woman, or a woman during her menstrual period abstained from sex. In other words, Native southerners had to forgo sexual intercourse for a far greater percentage of their lives than Europeans.

Furthermore, there were inappropriate venues for sex. Although a Native couple might engage in sex in a room occupied by others,

16. Lawson, *New Voyage*, 57; Cadwallader Colden, *History of the Five Indian Nations of Canada which Are Dependent on the Provinces of New York* (1747; reprint, New York: Allerton Books, 1922), 1:xxxiii; Alexander Moore, ed., *Nairne's Muskogean Journals: The 1708 Expedition to the Mississippi River* (Jackson: University of Mississippi Press, 1988), 33, 45.

17. Seymour Feiler, ed., *Jean-Bernard Bossu's Travels in the Interior of North America, 1751–1762* (Norman: University of Oklahoma Press, 1962), 131–32; Lawson, *New Voyage*, 40.

there were places, such as agricultural fields, where amorous encounters were forbidden. Violation of this rule could have serious consequences. According to the trader James Adair, the Cherokees blamed a devastating smallpox epidemic in 1738 on "the adulterous intercourses of their young married people, who the past year, had in a most notorious manner, violated their ancient laws of marriage in every thicket, and broke down and polluted many of their honest neighbors bean-plots, by their heinous crimes, which would cost a great deal of trouble to purify again."[18] For many Native southerners, therefore, a "toss in the hay" would have been a serious offense.

Native peoples also had rules against incest, but they did not define incest in the same way Euro-Americans did. Intercourse or marriage with a member of a person's own clan, for example, was prohibited, and the penalty could be death. Clan membership, which included all individuals who could trace their ancestry back to a remote, perhaps mythical figure, often ran into the thousands and included many people whom Europeans would not have regarded as relatives. Consequently, the number of forbidden partners was far greater than the number under the European definition of incest. The Cherokees, for example, had seven clans. No one could marry into his or her own clan, nor was the father's clan an acceptable marriage pool. The result was that, for any given Cherokee, almost one-third of all Cherokees were off-limits as sexual partners.

Each Native people had particular rules regarding marriage and incest. Many societies permitted men to have more than one wife and to marry sisters. The effect was not necessarily the devaluation of women, as European observers often claimed. Some cultural anthropologists suggest, in fact, that sororal polygamy correlates positively with high female status.[19] In the Southeast where husbands lived with their wives, the marriage of sisters to the same man reduced the number of men in the household and strengthened the control of women over domestic life. As Morse suggested, sisters often wanted to share a husband just as they shared a house, fields, labor, and children.

Ignorant of Native rules, southern colonials tended to view

---

18. Adair, *Adair's History*, 244.
19. Alice Schlegel, *Male Dominance and Female Autonomy: Domestic Authority in Matrilineal Societies* (New Haven: Yale University Press, 1972), 87–88.

Native women as wanton woodland nymphs over whose sexuality fathers, brothers, and husbands could exercise little control. Many colonists took full advantage of the situation as they perceived it. Some evidence, however, suggests that southeastern Native women were not as amenable to sexual encounters as Europeans suggested. Louis Philippe's anecdote reveals a woman, however bold and uninhibited, rejecting a sexual advance. When women did engage in sexual activity, many of them probably succumbed to pressure or force rather than charm.

European culture at this time countenanced considerable violence against women. William Byrd's confidential account of surveying the boundary line between North Carolina and Virginia, for example, describes several episodes of sexual aggression. One young woman, he wrote, "wou'd certainly have been ravish't, if her timely consent had not prevented the violence." This cavalier attitude toward a woman's right to refuse sex characterized much interaction between Native women and Europeans. Race almost certainly exacerbated the situation. The records of the South Carolina Indian trade are replete with Native complaints of sexual abuse at the hands of Europeans. One trader "took a young Indian against her Will for his Wife," another severely beat three women including his pregnant wife whom he killed, and a third provided enough rum to a woman to get her drunk and then "used her ill."[20] Obviously, the women in these incidents were not the ones who were lascivious.

Some Native peoples came to regard sexual misbehavior as the most distinguishing feature of European culture. The Cherokee Booger Dance, in which participants imitated various peoples, portrayed Europeans as sexually aggressive, and the men playing that role chased screaming young women around the dance ground. As it turns out, from the Native perspective, the British colonists of the American South may not have been so terribly different from Columbus's men after all.

20. William K. Boyd, ed., *William Byrd's Histories of the Dividing Line betwixt Virginia and North Carolina* (Raleigh: North Carolina Historical Commission, 1929), 147–48; William L. McDowell, ed., *Journals of the Commissioners of the Indian Trade, Sept. 20, 1710–Aug. 29, 1718* (Columbia: South Carolina Archives Department, 1955), 4, 37; William L. McDowell, *Documents Relating to Indian Affairs, 1754–1765* (Columbia: University of South Carolina Press, 1970), 231.

The people who do stand in stark contrast are Native men. James Adair, a resident of the Chickasaw Nation and a trader throughout the Southeast, perhaps knew the region's Native cultures better than any other European in the eighteenth century. As the husband of a Chickasaw woman and an occasional member of Chickasaw war parties against the Choctaws, he wrote with authority that "the Indians will not cohabitate with women while they are out at war; they religiously abstain from every kind of intercourse, even with their own wives." While Adair believed, perhaps correctly, that the reason for a period of abstinence was religious, the implications for female captives were clear. "The French Indians," he wrote, "are said not to have deflowered any of our young women they captivated, while at war with us." Even the most bloodthirsty Native warrior, according to Adair, "did not attempt the virtue of his female captives," although he did not hesitate to torture and kill them. Even the Choctaws, whom Adair described as "libidinous," had taken "several female prisoners without offering the least violence to their virtue, till the time of purgation was expired." Adair could not, however, resist the temptation to slander the Choctaws, the Chickasaws' traditional enemy: "Then some of them forced their captives, notwithstanding their pressing entreaties and tears."[21]

Captivity narratives suggest Indian men raped very few, if any, women victims of colonial wars—"a very agreeable disappointment" in one woman's words.[22] Rules prohibiting intercourse immediately before and after going to war may have contributed to the absence of documented sexual violence, but Native views on female sexuality and autonomy may have been equally responsible. Indians apparently did not view sex as property or as one of the spoils of war.

Columbus's men do seem to have equated sex and material plunder. The accounts of the destruction of the Hispaniola settlement link his men's desire for women with a desire for gold. In perhaps a more subtle way, British colonists also considered women to be a form of property and found the Native men's lack of proprietary

---

21. Adair, *Adair's History*, 171–72.
22. James Axtell, *The European and the Indian* (New York: Oxford University Press), 183.

interest in their wives and daughters incomprehensible. It called into question the Indians' concept of property in general and paved the way for Europeans to challenge Native people's ownership of land. From the second decade of colonization in the South, wealth depended on the cultivation of land, and southerners found the argument that Indians had no notion of absolute ownership particularly compelling.

While Native southerners forcefully maintained their right to inhabit the land of their fathers, they did not, in fact, regard land ownership in quite the same way as the Europeans who challenged their rights to it. They fought for revenge rather than for territory, they held land in common, and they permitted any tribal member to clear and cultivate unused tracts. Land did not represent an investment of capital, and Native southerners did not sell out and move on when other opportunities beckoned. Indeed, the land held such significance for most of them that they suffered severe economic, social, and political disruption rather than part with it. In the 1820s and 1830s, frontiersmen, land speculators, and politicians joined forces to divest Native peoples of their land, and southern state governments and ultimately the federal government took up the aggressors' cause. White southerners made a concerted effort to force their Indian neighbors to surrender their lands and move west of Mississippi to new territory. What difference did it make, many whites asked, which lands the Indians occupied? With squatters encroaching on them, shysters defrauding them at every turn, and federal and state authorities unwilling to protect them, Native peoples in the South struggled desperately to retain their homelands. They did so for reasons as incomprehensible to Euro-Americans as the sexual behavior of Native women. People who objectified both land and sex had encountered people who did not.

Ultimately, Native southerners lost. Representatives of the large southern tribes—Cherokees, Chickasaws, Choctaws, Creeks, and Seminoles—signed treaties in which they agreed to move west to what is today eastern Oklahoma. Remnants of some of those tribes as well as other isolated Native communities simply retreated into the shadows and eked out a living on marginal land, while the cotton kingdom expanded onto the rich soil that Native peoples had surrendered. In the cotton kingdom, land was salable rather than sacred, and power not parity characterized sexual relationships.

In recent years we have come to admire Native sensitivity to the natural world and to compare ourselves unfavorably to Indians on environmental issues and attitudes toward the land. Columbus and Pocahontas probably thought about sex at least as often as they did ecology, but we seem incapable of recognizing that their views on sex might have been as different as their ideas about land use. Disney's recent movie *Pocahontas* merely perpetuates the notion that romantic love is a universal concept that transcends cultural bounds and has little connection with specific aspects of a culture. The film depicts Pocahontas not as the autonomous person she probably was, but as a subservient young woman submissive to her father, betrothed to the warrior Kocoum, and won by Smith. Pocahontas's love for Smith (and vice versa) resolves conflicts with the Indians, and the English presumably set about the task at hand. "Oh, with all ya got in ya, boys," Governor Ratclife sings, "dig up Virginia, boys." True love, of course, characterized neither the real relationship between Pocahontas and John Smith nor the dealings of Native women and European men. Instead of Disney's John Smith, most Native women really met Columbus. Perhaps in the American South, where Columbus and Pocahontas metaphorically collided so forcefully, we should expand our comparison of Native Americans and Europeans beyond environmental issues and consider the interactions between men and women. Then we might begin to make connections between the materialism and the exploitation that have characterized so much of southern history and sexual violence against women.

Experiencing the American Revolution

November 1994
Louisville, Kentucky

JEAN B. LEE

Last January, when Janet Coryell called and invited me to
address this annual meeting, I happened to be reading
Having Our Say, the engaging reminiscences of Sarah and
Elizabeth Delany, African American sisters who have
shared their lives with one another for more than one
hundred years. When Janet called, it seemed that she was
offering me the opportunity to "have my say" about a
subject that has fascinated me for most of my adult life:
the American Revolution. At first I was hesitant about
accepting her invitation, then did so for two reasons. My
book was in press, and as part of bringing closure to that
twelve-year project, I had been contemplating just how
much one southern county had taught me about the
Revolution as a whole. Second, I have long lamented that
the founding epoch of the nation, as presented to scholars
and the public, often seems rather flat and incomplete,
lacking in the drama and fullness that people actually experienced two centuries ago. And I have thought about
how that exciting fullness might be recovered. Thus,
thanks to Janet for offering me, like the Delany sisters, an
occasion to "have my say" and share some ideas with you.

So long as they lived, people who experienced the
American Revolution felt a profound sense of destiny
about it and assigned supreme importance to what their
generation had wrought. The correspondence of Revolutionary leaders is replete with such ideas: Benjamin
Rush's belief that the winning of Independence consti-

tuted merely "the first act of the great drama" of revolution; Thomas Jefferson's wish that the Declaration of Independence would "be to the world, what I believe it will be (to some parts sooner, to others later, but finally to all), the signal . . . to assume the blessings and security of self-government"; and James Madison's unshakable conviction that the American Union was "in the eyes of the world, a wonder" and that the Revolution itself "had no parallels in the annals of human society."

The impulse to elevate and venerate the Revolution was scarcely limited to luminaries but was evident among lesser folk. Thus, in 1791 the vestry of a country church in Maryland lauded "the late glorious revolution." Nor were reverential gestures confined to words, as attested in an outpouring of instrumental music celebrating military victories and the Fourth of July, and also in the singularly eloquent testimony of a Virginian who served in the Continental Army. After the war this man visited Revolutionary battlefields; from each he carried away a piece of wood. Toward the end of his life, while living in Bourbon County, Kentucky, he took the wood to a carpenter, and in due time the old soldier went to his grave in a coffin made from that wood—a coffin that bore silent witness to, and consecrated, a defining moment of his life.

This deep sense of the Revolution's significance—in individual lives and in national and world history—seems mostly lost to the citizenry of the United States today. Despite being the founding epoch of the nation, the Revolution does not even come close to matching that other great epoch in our history, the Civil War, in scholarly output, media attention, or public engagement. Few Americans today evince much awareness that members of the Revolutionary generation surely were the most creative political architects in the nation's history—architects who fashioned a unique version of self-government, radically vested political sovereignty in ordinary people, wrote a bevy of constitutions and bills of rights at a rate probably never equaled before or since, and, to their own surprise, created the first modern political parties. Nor does one encounter widespread public awareness today that the Revolution began a process of social change that transformed American society and has yet to run its course—not least by disestablishing churches and trusting individual religious conscience, by linking white women's parenting responsibilities to the welfare of the young republic, and by recognizing (although not resolving) the jarring contradiction between founding a nation on principles of human liberty, yet keeping more than half a million black people enslaved. Finally, Americans today seem to have little appreciation that theirs was the first successful anticolonial revolution in modern world history; that it touched off a wave of revolution that between 1789 and 1848 washed over France, engulfed much of Western Europe, and reached the shores of Latin America; and that in the twentieth century the American experience inspired revolutionaries as diametrically opposite as Ho Chi Minh and Vaclav Havel.

One recent observation is emblematic: "To most Americans, the people and events surrounding the Revolution and the drafting of the Constitution feel wooden, formal and distant—a part of the country's remote past, and therefore unconnected to its modern experience"; "except for the basic facts learned in school, few Americans really know the full story of this momentous time." As if to underscore this point last July Fourth, a judge in New York used the following words to explain the importance of the Declaration of Independence to his ten-year-old son: "If you think about it . . . if these men had not made the contract they made over 200 years ago, we might not have hockey as we know it today." We are left with a trivialized Revolution, whose most common evocations are advertisements urging us to celebrate Washington's birthday by buying a used car, Fourth of July anniversaries largely devoid of meaningful connections to 1776, and politicians' attempts to legitimate their agendas by wrapping them in that all-purpose term, *patriotism.*

If commentary from the first half of the nineteenth century is correct, people began losing touch with the Revolution early, within a lifetime of the nation's founding. An aged Jefferson spoke of "a new generation whom we know not, and who know not us." Charles Francis Adams, writing in 1840, lamented that "the heroism of the females of the Revolution has gone from memory with the generation that witnessed it and nothing, absolutely nothing remains upon the ear of the young to the present day." Abraham Lincoln, speaking two years after the death of Madison, the last of the Founders, recognized that "the scenes of the revolution . . . like everything else . . . must fade upon the memory of the world, and grow more and more dim by the lapse of time."

But were the passing of time and the fading of memory alone

responsible for the descent into relative superficiality and obscurity? Certainly not. And among additional explanations that could be offered, I would emphasize three: the remarkable long-term *success* of the Revolution, how it was *remembered* in the nineteenth century, and how it has been *interpreted* in the twentieth century.

By many measures, the American Revolution proved to be astonishingly successful. What other modern revolutionary movement compares in creating stable representative government, encouraging the development of a more egalitarian society, establishing a military tradition of deference to civilian authority, and launching a nation on breathtaking economic and geographic expansion? What other revolution so early resulted, however contentiously and noisily, in the legitimation of political opposition and the peaceful transfer of power between adversaries—as happened in the United States by 1801? And what modern revolution had less to fear from entrenched counterrevolutionary forces?

So successful was the Revolution in establishing the American republic—and the Civil War in securing it—that it is easily taken for granted and seems virtually inevitable, as if the outcome were somehow foreordained. But that masks the tremendous task involved in creating a nation out of thirteen disparate and geographically dispersed colonies. As an English traveler noted in 1760, "Such is the difference of character, of manners, of religion, of interest, of the different colonies" that if "left to themselves, there would soon be a civil war from one end of the continent to the other." Early in the War of Independence, Nathanael Greene found Continental soldiers so attached to their localities that he wondered if Americans were capable of building a viable army. However much it may seem, in retrospect, that the success of the Revolution was inevitable, people at the time intimately experienced the uncertain, terrible messiness of revolutionary upheaval and warfare, without foreknowledge of the eventual outcome.

Unquestionably, the founding epoch would be remembered and commemorated, personally and publicly. Hence, as long as she lived, the daughter of a Virginia soldier kept her father's sword mounted over her bed. Obituaries mentioned battle scars that veterans bore to their graves. Fourth of July orations recalled "the noblest moment of our national glory." As the Revolutionary generation died off, Madison tried to impart "lessons of which posterity ought not to be deprived," while in 1825 Daniel Webster spoke for *his* generation as follows: "We can win no laurels in a war for independence. Earlier and worthier hands have gathered them all. . . . There remains to us the great duty of deference and preservation."

And so they did. Travelers regularly stopped at Mount Vernon and asked to be admitted to Washington's dank tomb. Shortly before the Civil War, by which time Mount Vernon was badly deteriorated, a group of southern women acquired the site with the intent of preserving it as a patriotic shrine. Enthusiastic autograph hunters traversed the country, trying to obtain a letter written by each of the signers of the Declaration of Independence or the Constitution. And biographies of Revolutionary leaders rolled off the printing presses.

As nineteenth-century Americans sought to preserve and venerate the past, however, they inevitably distorted it. Against a backdrop of rapid geographic expansion, economic and technological development, divisive sectionalism, explosive population growth, and a presumed need to assimilate millions of foreign-born immigrants who knew little of American history and institutions, the Revolution functioned as the bedrock of patriotism, a touchstone of national identity, a unifying element in a centripetal society rushing headlong toward an uncertain future. But as the founding epoch was put to these uses, it steadily lost authenticity. Symbolic, mythical iconography and narrative replaced much of the original complexity, contingency, and drama. Entire segments of the population (in fact, the majority) dropped from sight. African Americans simply disappeared. And rarely were white women's contributions recognized, probably because their politicization and their war efforts (including service as camp followers) offended nineteenth-century images of proper womanhood.

Even so, by the Civil War the memory of the Revolution, rather than unifying the nation, helped rend it asunder as southerners proclaimed the legacy of 1776 while northerners invoked the union of 1787. Lincoln's haunting wish in his first inaugural address, that the "mystic chords of memory, stretching from every [Revolutionary] battle-field, and patriot grave" would "yet swell the chorus of the Union," went unfulfilled, and after 1865 the sheer enormity and immediacy of the Civil War overwhelmed the memory of the earlier struggle, which slipped ever further into the realm of myth and symbol.

By the centennial of Independence, remember that the Revolution involved celebrating the deeds, real or imagined, of a pantheon of heroes—and a few heroines. The thousands of women who had traveled with the Continental Army were represented by one: the legendary Molly Pitcher, who risked her life by swabbing out cannons and replacing her husband when he fell in battle. Because of a flag that a mythologized Betsy Ross did not sew, of a design that is a nineteenth-century invention, she became more famous than Martha Washington. In the case of George Washington, veneration and even deification reached such heights that, according to one of his biographers, he became "a myth of suffocating dullness, the victim of civil elephantiasis." As the Revolution was more imaginatively celebrated than authentically remembered, it seemed to be personified not by real people but by cardboardlike figures—stiff, detached, and somehow unreal—and by encapsulating (perhaps fictional) phrases such as "Give me liberty or give me death."

As if to quell a fear voiced by Revolutionary leaders, that an adequate and accurate history of the nation's origins would never be written, scholars over the last century have labored mightily. They have probed ever more deeply the period's accomplishments and shortcomings, and its complex blend of intellectualism and raw emotion, hope and despair. The leading modern bibliographer of Revolutionary America estimates that, since 1876, well over one hundred thousand books, articles, and dissertations have appeared. Do we now have a reasonably balanced, comprehensive understanding of the Revolution? I think not—not yet. For the corpus of modern scholarship, notwithstanding its richness and sophistication, is also imbalanced, lacking in proportion, and, interpretively, too narrowly focused.

I am uncomfortable making broad generalizations without substantiating them, but let me offer a few. To begin, the major interpretations are strikingly bipolar. Was the Revolution fundamentally political and intellectual—a revolution of ideas? Or was it social and economic—a contest within America between competing groups for status and power? These questions have long dominated the discussion and shaped what we teach. It is as if historians have faith that some *primal essence* can be distilled from an upheaval that engulfed a population of more than 2 million people. Just as the poles of a magnet radiate lines of force, the bipolarity of the scholarship has created a rather narrow band of overarching questions and interpretations.

In addition, the historical literature suffers from a remarkable lack of proportion. For example, much greater attention has been devoted to the coming of the Revolution rather than its consequences—with the exception of national political development. There is an unfortunate, untenable tendency to present New England, the smallest and least representative region, as a surrogate for the national experience. We know far more about politics *in* America than the war *for* America. And during the last quarter century, attention has been lavished on ideas and ideology to the neglect of both action and the contexts in which ideas developed and were expressed.

Bernard Bailyn's *The Ideological Origins of the American Revolution,* published in 1967, was so influential that he bequeathed the succeeding generation of investigators a near obsession with the role of ideology in shaping the new nation. It became the kudzu of Revolutionary scholarship. Yet, as this approach seemed to draw in and overrun everything in its path, critics railed against "disembodied ideology" that treated what people *said* apart from what they *did.* Meanwhile, practitioners fell into endless, increasingly esoteric, and irreconcilable debate. What originally had been billed as the republican synthesis soon shattered into competing interpretations and in time produced the bipolarity of corporatist republicanism versus individualistic liberalism. "This disagreement among historians," Robert Shalhope has warned, "threatens to cloud our understanding of the formative years of the nation's past. Certainly, Americans living in these years never felt themselves confronted by two sharply contrasting modes of thought." In a similar vein, Pauline Maier recently observed that "the distinctions drawn by modern historians were all but irrelevant to eighteenth-century Americans." One wonders whether the liberalism-republicanism dialogue reveals more about the culture of the contemporary academy than the culture of Revolutionary America.

A character in one of Janet Peery's short stories complains of people who, in trying to fit things into boxes, leave important parts out. With regard to the Revolutionary period, what has been left out? How might we achieve a richer, more comprehensive history? Doubtless, every specialist could produce her or his own list, complete with qualifying references to the historiography. High on my list would be three items: time, place, and war.

First, time. Much of the scholarship fragments the period. Instead of treating the time span from the late colonial years to the early nineteenth century as a whole, most studies begin or end somewhere in the middle: especially at Independence, the end of the war, or establishment of the federal government. But unless we follow one generation's passage from colonial status *through* political upheaval and war, to at least 1800, the Revolution's immense transforming power cannot be fully grasped. Compelling proof of the value of this approach lies, of course, in the field of women's history.

Conversely, a more compartmentalized, chronologically sensitive treatment of slavery is overdue. The typical focus of academic discussion remains rather narrow: namely, indictment (occasionally defense) of the founding generation for not doing more to eradicate human bondage. If one takes the long view, however, and recognizes that servile labor systems were thousands of years old and endemic across much of the globe, then what seems remarkable is *not* that slavery was not abolished throughout the new nation, but how rapidly, during just one generation, it created deep crosscurrents and ultimately unbearable tensions.

Consider, too, the perceptions and attitudes of black people who lived during the latter half of the eighteenth century. For the colonial period, little surviving evidence admits us to their interior world; most of what is known dates from the years after the colonies started down the road to Independence. Still, it is worth asking how slaves conceived of their condition during the colonial period, when some whites also were held in servitude, when the civil, political, and religious liberties of a majority of women and men were significantly circumscribed, and when memories of Africa probably included memories of African slavery. Did daily existence in bondage become more burdensome once Thomas Jefferson proclaimed that all men were created equal, slavery became an explosive political and moral issue, and the growth of free black populations offered an alternative vision of existence? Not only are there no clear answers to these questions, but we seldom ask the questions. And that reduces historians' capacity to probe more deftly the Revolution's transformative powers.

Just as important as the question of time (when the narrative begins and ends) is the matter of place: the geographic and cultural regions and communities in which people lived. Thorough examination of discrete places can illuminate large themes with reassuring particularity. Charles Joyner, contemplating antebellum slavery, takes historians to task for *not* paying closer attention to place.

> All history is local history, somewhere. And yet how little this obvious fact is reflected in the scholarship. . . . Historians describe *the* slave community without having probed in depth any *particular* slave community. A bit of this from Virginia and a little of that from Texas, seasoned with a pinch of something else from Mississippi, have been presented as a portrait of the slave South. . . . Too many scholars . . . attempt to describe and analyze abstract wholes without having investigated concrete parts. Too few construct wholes from empirically researched parts. . . . No history, properly understood, is of merely local significance.

So, too, with the Revolution. Everyone, *everywhere*, experienced and was affected by the immense changes that swept across America beginning in the 1760s. Yet, little is known about how the majority of Americans, *in their communities*, were drawn into the vortex, endured the longest war in American history, adjusted to wrenching dislocations associated with leaving the British Empire, and simultaneously vested themselves in a new nation. Historians' sense of place is also skewed toward urban centers and New England, which by definition neglects the South. True, urban centers often served as flash points of resistance and conflict, but less than a tenth of the American population lived there. And without the support of rural communities, which frequently toned down the radicalism of town dwellers, the Revolution never would have succeeded.

Then there is the problem of New England, a problem not limited to the eighteenth century. I mean the tendency to interpret whatever happened in that region, especially in Massachusetts, as normative, thereby establishing a standard against which the rest of the nation is judged, and often judged deficient. In fact, a New England perspective can be a peculiar one. Nowhere else, for example, did patriots display such genius at provoking the British and then, when imperial authorities reacted, loudly proclaiming to be innocent victims of tyranny. Peculiar, too, is the claim that republicanism, with its roots in the classical world, was a secular version of Puritanism. And however much John Adams believed in the superiority of New Englanders' laws, morals, manners, and even countenances, that opinion found little acceptance outside the region. Witness an epithet printed in a New York newspaper in 1770, that Boston was "the common sewer of America," or Washington's comment, shortly after he arrived in Massachusetts in the summer of 1775, that the locals "are an exceedingly dirty and nasty people."

With considerations of time and place much in mind, in 1981 I decided to examine the Revolutionary experience of one southern society. Some years earlier, I had visited Charles County, Maryland, bordering the Potomac River. Never before had I been able to situate myself so well—both physically and in my imagination—in the eighteenth century. Revolutionary-period maps guided me from place to place because not much had changed in two hundred years. Standing in a graveyard overlooking the Potomac and its luxuriant shoreline, I could easily imagine how *quiet* the earlier county must have been. That impression was confirmed when I discovered that local people heard the cannonade at the Battle of Yorktown, one hundred miles to the south. Any southern county with good records could have served as the site for my investigation, but I never considered any place except this place, where the landscape so evoked another time.

On the eve of Independence, Charles County was home to about sixteen thousand people. It was a quintessential Chesapeake tidewater county, with a hierarchical social order extending from gentry to slaves, and an agricultural economy based on tobacco and foodstuffs, and lines of trade extending to the West Indies, Europe, and Africa. Port Tobacco, the county seat, was the busiest town on the Maryland side of the river.

Because I intended to examine the entire society, it would be necessary to use both traditional sources and some of the social history methodology that recently had so enriched the field of early colonial history. But from the beginning I intended that methodology to undergird, not overwhelm, what would be a coherent narrative of revolution and war. There was just one problem: I had no idea whether such a narrative could be constructed from the voluminous public records but rather sparse private records that have survived.

Only after about five years of research could I begin to see the outlines of a narrative. Then gradually, over seven more years of research and writing, a vibrant but largely forgotten world emerged.

Let me share with you a few glimpses of that world, beginning with a woman named Ann Halkerston. In 1762 she was a "distressed" widow with three young sons and no relatives to assist her. Several members of the gentry came forward and organized a charitable lottery to help her become financially solvent. Soon she was the proprietor of a well-frequented tavern (Thomas Jefferson stayed there in 1775, while on his way to the Continental Congress at Philadelphia). By the time she died in 1777, Ann Halkerston owned seven slaves and could afford to send a son abroad to be educated.

As an economically independent woman who remained *feme sole* for many years, Halkerston does not fit conventional images of white female dependency in early America. And she was not alone, for a substantial group of single, property-holding women lived in Charles County. Some were spinsters; the majority were widows. Their fortunes typically began not in charitable acts, as in Halkerston's case, but in bequests from parents and husbands or in shrewd claims to dower rights. In economic terms, these women were among the most marriageable in the county, yet they chose the freedom of *feme sole* rather than the civil death of coverture. They could afford to do so because they controlled land and/or slave labor. By 1790 some of the largest slaveholders in the county were white women.

Members of this group, who eschewed marriage and maintained economic independence, therefore represent a counterpoint to female dependency in early America. They were not like women in the seventeenth-century Chesapeake, who apparently almost always became planters' wives, marrying and remarrying, quickly, because they had little alternative. Nor were they like many New England widows, who were forced to live dependent, constricted lives, usually in adult children's households, because they could not farm by themselves. A more telling comparison would be *signares*, women of the African and Brazilian coasts who profited from owning and trading slaves during the era of the transatlantic trade. In Charles County, as in other slave societies around the Atlantic rim, unfree labor sustained the economic well-being of women who were more autonomous than most others in those societies.

Location was as important *within* the vast Chesapeake region as in the wider Atlantic world. Recent work on pre-Revolutionary Maryland and Virginia emphasizes deep social stress and a threatened gentry, owing to challenges from evangelical Protestants and nascent democrats or, alternatively, anxiety over indebtedness to English merchants. None of these factors seems to have been operative in Charles County. Rather, its late colonial society was distinguished by stability and a secure, self-confident gentry leadership.

Then revolution and war fell across the land, and enormous change came to the county in just a few years. As engines of change, the Revolution and the War for Independence were inseparably entwined, each reinforcing and amplifying the other. Although only warfare secured the Independence and nationhood proclaimed on parchment in 1776, in most of the historical literature the war is cordoned off from the rest of the Revolutionary experience. That, as John Shy once observed, "is essentially false to the historical event, because people living through the long, hard years from 1775 to 1783 made no such artificial distinction." The war also cast a long shadow over subsequent American development. Yet, in Fred Anderson's words, "failure to understand the enormous consequences of warfare . . . is the most persistent problem—and the greatest challenge—facing historians of the American Revolution today."

Charles County was never the site of a major battle. British forces never occupied territory there, as they did in Charleston and New York. Nor was the county ever the scene of horrific guerrilla warfare, as in the Carolinas. Even so, local people were thoroughly caught up in the long conflict: it placed unprecedented demands on them to support the Continental Army with troops and materials and to defend seventy-five miles of Potomac shoreline from British naval raiding. After 1783 legacies of the war caused as much change and suffering as the war itself.

However much Washington and Continental officers complained about the public's failure to adequately support the army, the experiences of Charles County people tell a different story. True, enthusiasm waxed and waned, individual efforts ranged from grudging to generous, but on balance the record of accomplishment was impressive. So many local men served as Continental soldiers that by 1780 the county reportedly was "much pillaged" of its youth. All the while, planting families and their slaves produced material. Outfitting and feeding the military were new and extremely complicated undertakings, which required coordination among the army, Congress, state governments, and the localities where supply lines began. In Charles County, urgent requests for supplies often arrived without warning, and trying to fill requisitions seemed akin to shooting at a moving target. One month the item most urgently wanted might be blankets, the next wheat, then flour or horses. By the time people could react to one crisis, it might have subsided but the next would be at hand. More than once, people made military priorities their own, then were disappointed when the army no longer required what it had urgently requested. Despite these difficulties, people persevered, and as the war reached its climax in 1781, they worked at a feverish pace. That summer and early autumn, they produced thousands of bushels of wheat and hundreds of head of cattle on the hoof for the Yorktown campaign.

Serving in and supplying the army surely were the most tangible ways in which ordinary Americans vested themselves in the new nation. During the first years of the United States—war years—only two national institutions existed: Congress and the Continental Army. Congress was a distant entity, with no direct ties to the citizenry. The army, on the other hand, was filled with fathers, husbands, and sons and augmented with women and children. Charles County people attached to the army traveled over hundreds of miles of unfamiliar territory, passed through towns they had never heard of, fought at places like Camden and Guilford Courthouse, and encountered everything from Yankee accents to Carolina drawls. They saw, with their own eyes, the expanse and potential of the country, and they risked their lives for it. Even for those who never left the county, the war offered tangible ways in which they, too, might identify with the nation. Thus, women who sewed shirts and knit stockings knew that the work of their hands would warm soldiers' bodies, just as planters understood that grain from their fields would ease the army's hunger.

Identification with the national cause was not the only way in which the war changed life in the county. Recruiting and training soldiers, producing materials, and defending against British raiding called forth unprecedented levels of communal organization and cooperation. After 1783 inhabitants turned their energies to rebuilding a war-ravaged economy and bettering themselves and their society. Even when they resumed projects laid aside during the war, such as education and economic development, the scope of their efforts often was broader, more ambitious, than in the colonial period. The war seems to have taught them, as nothing else had, the value of organized collective undertakings. Much has been made of the importance of voluntary associations in the early republic. More needs to be made of the role of the war, with its unprecedented impetus for communal action, in contributing to the growth of voluntarism.

Alongside the positive consequences of the war, it also exacted a tremendous price in Charles County. War devastated the agricultural economy, and peace did not restore its vitality. In no small part because of a huge public war debt, civil government nearly collapsed in the 1780s and remained moribund into the 1790s. A surprising number of elite men, as well as some of the property-holding unmarried women, sank into insolvency. And black family and communal ties were disrupted as whites desperate for liquidity rapidly sold off slaves, some of whom remained in the area, others of whom were taken away. Meanwhile, owing to the favorable peace treaty, millions of acres of western land beckoned to the propertied and the poor, as did the rising towns of Alexandria, Washington, and Baltimore. The result was massive out-migration until, on the eve of the Civil War, the county's population was 20 percent less than when Washington became president. Whereas colonial travelers had described inviting scenes, postwar travelers saw abandoned plantations, impoverishment, and a population in the process of shifting to a black, enslaved majority. Thus, the price of nationhood came high in Charles County. Its people would not have recognized themselves in modern interpretations that deny the frighteningly unstable character of the postwar years, or that downplay the revolutionary nature of the Revolution.

We know so little about other communities, especially southern communities, that it is impossible to say how typical or exceptional were the experiences of people in the county. What *is* well established is that the southern colonies, because of their commodity crops and Atlantic-trade links, constituted the most valuable sector of the British Empire. Independence and the war shattered the imperial relationship and sharply curtailed commercial opportunities during the postwar years. In addition, the South sustained the high-est per capita cost of the war and the most widespread destruction. Quite possibly, therefore, the South also faced the most difficult postwar recovery of any region in the United States. Surely, these circumstances helped shape southerners' memories of the Revolu-tion—and their sense of themselves in the new nation. As we learn more about these developments, our understanding of the capa-cious founding epoch, and of southern identities, will advance exponentially.

Unfinished Business

ANNE FIROR SCOTT

November 1995
New Orleans, Louisiana

In this age of electronic miracles somehow the list of proposed titles I sent to Kathleen Berkeley never arrived in Wilmington, and so she made up a title that turns out to be better than any I had proposed.

"Unfinished business" is, of course, the central characteristic of our discipline. "History," meaning the history we write and read and talk about, is always changing as new evidence turns up, as new questions are asked. Unfinished business is also an appropriate subject for a person my age seeking to understand what she has been about for fifty years.

I propose to talk principally about the first meaning, that is, the changing nature of women's history over time, and then just a little about the second. But first, given the present alarms and confusions in our discipline, I should try to say where I stand. After listening to many heated discussions I conclude that I am a moderate postmodernist, if there is such a thing. By that I mean that I do believe that each of us sees the past through a prism created by our own life experience. I observe that historical evidence is perceived differently by different people in different contexts. How historians define history and what they choose to write about are also in part a function of their cultural milieu and the concepts and language available to them.

However—and this may mean that my claim to be a sort of modified postmodernist will not do—I believe that real things happened to real people, to nations, to societies and cultures, that an all-seeing eye could discern. But since no eye is all-seeing, we "construct" what we write from the materials at hand. However, the building blocks of that construction, if we are conscientious about evidence, are approximations of reality. I also believe that however useful theoretical structures may be, conclusions must follow from the evidence whether or not they fit the theory.

My basic argument today will be that from the beginning, women's history developed in close association with women's activism, and that the two continually influenced each other. That interactive process has accelerated to the point that what was once a thin trickle of writing is now a veritable torrent. I also propose to argue that from the beginning women's history followed a separate track from the grand narratives of the American past created by male historians.

When I began thinking about the essay last summer I was rereading Jane Austen's *Northanger Abbey*. Some of you have discovered that marvelous paragraph in which the heroine responds to a young man who is urging her to read history: " 'I read it a little as a duty,' says Catherine Moorland, 'but it tells me nothing that does not either vex or weary me. The quarrels of popes and kings, with wars and pestilence in every page; the men all so good for nothing and hardly any women at all, it is very tiresome.' "

It occurred to me that Jane Austen was a younger contemporary of Mary Wollstonecraft—though it may be doubted that they ever heard of each other—and that each in her own way was responding to a current of thought that was emerging into popular consciousness in the late eighteenth century.

Even before Wollstonecraft and Austen began writing, interesting things were happening across the sea in Massachusetts, where Judith Sergeant Murray was drawing examples from women's history to support her argument for expanding women's opportunity for education.

A few years later Hannah Mather Crocker's *Observations on the Real Rights of Women* also used historical examples to support her view that mind had no sex. In the 1830s Lydia Maria Child's two-volume *History of the Condition of Women in Various Ages and Nations* and Sarah Grimké's *Letters on the Equality of the Sexes* used women's historical experience to build their arguments for women's emancipation.

While these ambitious women were writing history, many others were reading it. As early as 1803, a six-volume work, *Female Biography*, edited by a woman, published in London, began to circulate in the United States. Over the next sixty years British and American publishers brought out a whole series of fat volumes containing biographies of women ranging from Eve to contemporaries, compiled from all sorts of sources, biblical and classical as well as various standard history books. In 1844 Samuel Goodrich, who made his living writing historical and didactic works for a general market, published *Lives of Celebrated Women*, which he introduced with the following sentence: "It may indeed be true that the happiness of women is generally to be found in the quiet domestic circle, but that all without distinction should be confined to it, and that whenever one of the sex departs from it she departs from her allotted sphere, is not more true than a similar proposition would be of men."

A decade later the author of a book called *Noble Deeds of American Women* boasted that it had sold eight thousand copies in two years and that the demand required a second edition. In 1855 the prolific editor of *Godey's Ladies Book*, Sarah Josepha Hale, brought out *Woman's Record from Creation to 1854*. Until at least 1874, she published successive editions, moving the closing date forward year after year.

These compilers of women's history borrowed freely from each other and did not always distinguish clearly between documented fact and legend. Heroine worship was rife, and part of the purpose was to inspire the young, to provide what we would today call role models.

Only one of these early writers, Elizabeth Ellett, came close to understanding modern standards of evidence. Seeking to document women's part in the American Revolution she lamented the scarcity of documents as she searched out unpublished letters and interviewed descendants of Revolutionary women. Her experiments with oral history and her interest in ordinary women foreshadowed the social history of our own day.

I believe that the women who bought these books were beginning to question their own status and were seeking reinforcement from the historical record. There is a good deal of evidence for this proposition. By the 1830s the phrase "women's rights" was cropping up in correspondence and in print, sometimes in unexpected places. A young woman at the Troy Female Seminary announced that she had bought a "large square notebook" in which she proposed to write everything she could find about women's past. Troy offered no course in women's history, but Emma Willard, behind her conservative and very ladylike facade, was a passionate feminist. While she herself did not publicly support suffrage, many of her pupils grew up to become vigorous advocates of women's rights. The woman of the square notebook not only became an ardent suffragist but also would show up nearly sixty years later giving a lecture on the history of women at the Columbian Exposition. These were also the years of Margaret Fuller's famous "Conversations"—I am tempted to call them the first graduate seminar in America—many of which focused on women's history and women's status. Then in 1845 came Fuller's *Woman in the Nineteenth Century*, a landmark in the development of thinking on the subject.

In these same years more and more young women were finding their way to education and women's voluntary associations—many of them devoted to reform were literally all over the map. In their own societies women were inventing ways to exercise community power. They learned to speak in public, to handle money, to knock on doors in search of signatures to petitions, to lobby legislatures. Both young women in the seminaries and their mothers in voluntary associations were forging new roles for themselves and looking to women's history for guidance.

Meanwhile, of course, gifted amateurs were writing the broader history of the United States of the Americas. Professional historians as we know them did not exist. Men such as George Bancroft, Francis Parkman, and William Prescott, for example, were self-trained scholars, diligent in research, whose definition of history, though often broad, did not include any interest in what women had been or done. The assumption that men made history was so deeply ingrained that they were quite unaware that they held it. Though women's history was developing rapidly, it remained on a separate track.

Many women displayed a nascent historical consciousness that led them to make records of their own experience. How in the world women crossing the country in covered wagons found time, not to mention paper and ink, I cannot imagine. But write they did, as masses of documents testify. The Civil War, like the westward movement, inspired many women, North and South, to keep diaries and journals.

In 1876 Elizabeth Cady Stanton and Susan B. Anthony set themselves the formidable task of documenting the history of the woman suffrage movement that they had done so much to create. Their first volume was an eclectic assortment of historical documents by and about women drawn from many sources. In time they and their successors would produce six volumes of what we now see as indispensable primary sources: *The History of Woman Suffrage.*

While they wrote, in the 1870s and 1880s, women's associations were proliferating all around them. Woman suffrage became a part of the national political debate, complete with congressional hearings and the introduction of a constitutional amendment. These years also brought another flood of biographical books. In one of these, published in 1880, the editor wrote, "it is impossible as we pass from one sketch to another not to be reminded of the glorious women of all ages and countries about whom next to nothing is known. Here history has indeed been unjust. . . ."

Later, in a curious foreshadowing of Virginia Woolf's famous meditation on Shakespeare's sister, we read about Sarah Fielding, gifted sister of the novelist Henry: "We do not know what became of her. Most likely she was obliged to leave her novel writing and Greek translations in order to make shirts, pastry and gooseberry wine." One imaginative editor asked contemporary women of achievement to write essays about each other—a fascinating volume in which we learn as much about the authors as about their subjects.

From women's perspective the high point of the 1890s was the Columbian Exposition. Women from all over the world came to Chicago to view the multiple exhibits in the Women's Building and to exchange ideas. Women's speeches fill three fat volumes. Hundreds of women spoke, and many talked about the history of women in order to make contemporary points.

In the 1890s, too, numerous local women's groups combined to form national associations, and these in turn accelerated the compilation of data. Jane Croly, convinced that the widespread founding of women's clubs constituted the major social movement of her time, set out to make a record of what club women were accomplishing. Her *History of the Woman's Club Movement in America*, like *The History of Woman Suffrage*, provides a mass of data for the present-day historian to deconstruct.

At approximately the same time Gertrude Mossell broadened the scope of women's history with her *Work of Afro-American Women*. She was clear about her purpose: "That some note of inspiration might be found in these writings for the budding womanhood of the race. . . ." She provided information about an impressive list of black women of achievement in education, literature, journalism, medicine, law, missionary work, art, business, and music, as well as the "uncrowned queens of the fireside." Mixed with her records of accomplishment were evocative discussions of the pain of what she called "caste in institutions."

Still another valuable collection of data grew out of a project paid for by Mrs. Russell Sage. This one involved sending a questionnaire to every woman for whom an address could by found who had spent any time at the Troy Female Seminary. For women no longer alive, queries went to descendants or friends or even to postmasters. The original questionnaires have survived and are possibly the largest exhibition collection of data about nineteenth-century middle-class women of some education.

In yet another ambitious effort, Frances Willard and Mary Livermore collected biographies often written (at least one would guess from internal evidence) by the women themselves and encompassing a wide variety of political and social activists and a large number of writers. These essays, like those in the Troy volume, provide an excellent source for reconstructing the self-images of achieving women at the turn of the century.

While women were emerging in so many ways that the nineteenth century would often be labeled "the woman's century," a great change was taking place in the intellectual world generally and partially in the definition of history as a discipline. In 1876 Johns Hopkins University had inaugurated a seminar in American history on the German model. By 1887 men who had graduated from this or other such seminars established the American Historical Association and began to lay down the rules for the study and writing of history. Very soon students (including some women) were taking the Ph.D. in history at Harvard, Yale, Princeton, Chicago, Wisconsin, and Berkeley. Yet the books these newly minted scholars wrote, no matter what the subject, had no place for women at all.

Women's history continued as it had begun on its separate path, still closely tied to women's activism. In 1914 a scholar appeared who was to do as much as anyone to shape the next phase. Mary Beard's *Women's Work in the Municipalities* was yet another attempt to record the changing social and political roles of women, but this time by a woman who, though she had dropped out of graduate school, had made herself into a professional historian. Mary Beard was young, thirty-eight, and at the beginning of what would become a long career in historical writing closely tied to political concerns. In the 1920s she collaborated with her husband to write *The Rise of American Civilization,* one of the most widely read general works in American history ever published, and one in which women were treated seriously. For once the separate paths converged. It would not happen again for many years.

Mary Beard became a crusader for the preservation of women's history. In the 1930s she embarked on an ambitious project to establish a world center for the collection of women's papers and the study of women's history. The project aroused much enthusiasm, but the depression was deepening and money was very scarce. Despite brave beginnings, the project as she conceived it failed. Its broad outlines, however, were destined to reappear in the 1940s with the establishment of the Women's Archives at Radcliffe, precursor of today's Schlesinger Library.

In three more books, *Understanding Women, America through Women's Eyes,* and *Women as Force in History* (published in 1931, 1933, and 1940, respectively), Beard set the agenda for much that would follow. Along the way she endlessly urged women's colleges to rethink their curricula, to reshape them around what we would today call women's studies. Nobody was yet ready to hear what she was saying. (I hope everybody here has read or will read Nancy Cott's wonderful collection of Mary Beard's letters.)

Meantime, what was going on in the South? Here, too, women were beginning, albeit a little later than in the Northeast, to be energized in their own behalf. First in missionary societies and the WCTU, then in the YWCA and in clubs, and finally—after 1910—in a vigorous suffrage movement southern women began to develop a significant public life.

Scholarly history was not far behind. The first sign came in the 1920s when, for reasons now lost to sight, a young woman studying at the University of Wisconsin decided to write her dissertation on the subject of antebellum southern women. Virginia Gearhart had been an honor student at Goucher, a school notable for faculty women with a strong community orientation. Gearhart, a Marylander, thought of herself as a southerner, and her pioneering research is punctuated now and then with familiar southern mythology. Still, she made a brave beginning.

In the 1930s two first-rate scholars, Julia Cherry Spruill and Guion Griffis Johnson, and two others whose work was impressive, Margery Mendenhall and Eleanor Boatwright, published in the field. Though all five of these women wrote important scholarly articles or books illuminating the history of southern women, as far as I can tell, none of the work had the slightest impact on those who controlled the teaching and writing of southern history. Not only was their excellent scholarship almost entirely ignored, but not one was able to find an academic post worthy of her talents. Each worked out such accommodations as she could at the time. Boatwright and Mendenhall were cut off in their prime, one by suicide, the other by a medical error. Of the three who lived a normal life span, one spent her life as a manuscript librarian, one as an organizer of women's associations (though she continued into her eight- ` ies writing good historical articles), and one as a *Christian Science* reader. Their scholarship had been excellent, but they were women, and theirs was an area not yet recognized by the gatekeepers as a legitimate field of study.

Fortunately, the printed word does not perish as readily as the people who write it, and much of this work was destined to reappear when there were people ready to listen. This came in the 1960s.

The atmosphere had been changing for a long time, but World War II—as it did so many things—accelerated the change in women's opportunities. More and more southern women were going to college and into the labor force. It was a sign of the times that the League of Women Voters grew rapidly in the South, and by the early 1950s league members were joining southern white church women in actively preparing for school integration.

In 1961 a paper on southern women's history appeared for the first time on the program of this august association. It was my good fortune to have come upon evidence for the post–Civil War emergence of southern women just in the nick of time to be—so to speak—present at the creation.

Nine years went by before the book foreshadowed by that paper finally came out—only a step ahead, as it turned out, of what would become an avalanche of work on the subject. This acceleration of interest reflected the continuing change in the context: by 1970 young southern women had been exhilarated and energized by the civil rights movement. The gentle breeze that preceded the hurricane of feminism had begun to blow. Numbers of women began to enter history graduate programs, boldly proposing to study the history of their own sex.

So it came to be that the subject that had merited three citations in the index of the Link and Patrick bibliographical volume in 1968 filled more than fifty pages in its successor, edited by John Boles and Evelyn Nolen in 1987. I wonder if any new field in the discipline has ever grown so rapidly. Like our predecessors, we twentieth-century historians of women have been profoundly concerned with social and political issues and with our own status. For this reason, more than in most other subfields of American history, our books, even at their most scholarly, speak to women who are not historians.

We may have reached a point at which the study of women's history has become self-propelling, perhaps less dependent on a favorable context; for though feminism itself is under attack and often declared to be dead—a rumor that is vastly exaggerated—books, articles, monographs, and panels appear with unabated enthusiasm. The field continues to grow both in substance—new questions are constantly being raised, new groups and individuals being studied—and in theoretical sophistication. Some of the things that are going on now—for example, the strong emphasis upon theory, a good deal of crossover from literary criticism, the extraordinary burgeoning of black women's history, the ever increasing interest in lower-class women, farmers' wives, and the like—might lead us to ask what elements in American culture just now encourage these developments, but that is a question for some future panel.

For the moment, perhaps, it is enough to say that over its long history—since Judith Sergeant Murray began to draft her essays in

1776—women's history in this country has developed in close relationship with women's activism and has itself affected that activism, providing the inspiration and encouragement for many
efforts to broaden women's world. Also from the beginning it has
run on its own track, ignored by the so-called mainstream (mostly
male) historians. The first characteristic continues to this day and
perhaps accounts in part for the extraordinary amount of work we
have done since 1960. The second is, I believe, beginning to change.
Perhaps the day is not far distant when every scholar working in a
relevant field will pay close attention to women's records as well as
those created by men.

Examining nearly seventy years of historiography, one finds that
the notion that history is always unfinished is not hard to grasp. But
we must not forget that what we are doing today will be seen as
equally unfinished fifty years from now. Historians writing over the
years have done the best they knew how (and we should not for a
moment suggest that they were any less intelligent or perceptive
than we are). We write by our lights, as they did by theirs. I was
struck the other day by a comment Charles Darwin made to his
friend and codiscoverer of natural selection, Alfred Russell Wallace:
"the firmest conviction of the truth of a doctrine by its author seems,
alas, not to be the slightest guarantee of its truth." Many of the formulations that seem to us so exactly to tell the truth about the past
will probably be discarded by the next generation of scholars on the
basis of new evidence, new insight, new theories.

Turning now for just a few moments to my own experience with
"unfinished business," when I consulted my historian daughter as
to what shape this talk ought to take, she said, "Well, be autobiographical but not too much." So I shall try to follow her advice.

A friend my age said the other day, "Everybody is writing memoirs; I think it's the word processor!" I think, rather, it is a stage of
life. In one's first four or five decades everything seems to lie ahead:
discoveries, articles, books. But the time comes when so much more
lies behind than can possibly lie ahead, and many of us are driven
to try to make sense of our own experience as we have for years
been trying to make sense of other people's.

Striving to write a truthful afterword for the twenty-fifth-
anniversary edition of *The Southern Lady*, I asked myself how I came
to write this book. What influences came to bear? I tried to think

back. Growing up in the 1920s I was surrounded by southern women, some of whom considered themselves ladies. As children must, I absorbed the prevailing ambiance, the tones of voice, the off-hand comments of grown-ups. Once I referred to a black woman as a lady and was reproved. Long after her death I discovered that my grandmother, whose picture appears on the cover of the new edition, fitted almost exactly the description I had drawn in the manuscripts of well-to-do, highly respectable southern girls who yearned for education, made do with what they could persuade their parents to provide, and created careers in church work and voluntary associations. She went to a teachers' college, married young, had five children, was a pillar of her church, helped some black women set up a day-care center, and—after suffrage—traveled to Georgia to organize the new branches of the League of Women Voters.

She did not like to keep house, my mother said, but loved to read and write. She was not permitted by her patriarchal father-in-law to sign the articles she wrote for the local paper, but had enough independence to stay with her own church instead of joining her husband's. There were others who shaped my understanding of southern women: my mother and her sister, who were full of family stories about their patriarchal grandfather, four of my college teachers, a black woman who came to nurse my little brothers and then went to college and came home to teach school.

Much of this effort to unravel my own past as it fits into the larger past is in the afterword of this book, but I am sure I have only skimmed the surface. How, I asked myself as I struggled to tell the truth, if it is so difficult to reconstruct one's own past, does one dare to try to reconstruct that of other people? But we do try and we will continue to, but I hope with a certain tentativeness, a decent humility.

Do not think for a moment that this is a farewell address, for with a little bit of luck I shall be around to write at least one more book, to teach a few more students, edit a few more manuscripts, maybe even review a few more books. But since I may not have just this wonderful opportunity again I would like to say thank you for all the support, cooperation, praise—deserved or undeserved—that has come from so many of the people in this audience over the years. History is not only forever unfinished, but also forever a collective enterprise. The degree to which we can continue to see ourselves not as rivals but as collaborators will partly determine how much we are able to add to the sum of human knowledge and, what is more important, to add to our own satisfaction with life. So I thank you all, and look forward to shaking many hands at the reception to which you are all most urgently invited.

"But She Can't Find Her [V. O.] Key"

Writing Gender and Race into Southern Political History

November 1996
Little Rock, Arkansas

Each time we sit down to write, we yearn for the impossible: to clear our minds, to focus sharply, to be transported into our material and transformed into a person who can do justice to the passions and peculiarities of people of the past.[1] Sometimes, if we get really lucky, magic happens; we find a voice, stories spill out, arguments leap up into topic sentences, conclusions cohere. Just once in a while, Clio appears to guide us, and our very own muse makes the crooked places straight on the screen.

But more often, the antimuse plagues us. Demons provoke us, reminding us of daily duties gone begging, or pricking the fragile bubbles of confidence that float in our brains, ultimately sapping not just inspiration, but any sort of sense at all that might guide us to write the next paragraph. My own particular demons are crafty: they often take the form of half-remembered rock-and-roll lyrics, fragments of chirpy pop songs, originating far more often from South Philly than from Liverpool. These naked prefeminist homilies seek to convince me that while I might be masquerading as a historian, somewhere,

1. The title for this essay refers to V. O. Key, who wrote *Southern Politics in State and Nation* (New York: Alfred A. Knopf, 1949), the definitive work on southern political history for a generation.

deep inside, I am that early-1960s American teen, sitting by the phone, waiting for Bobby Darin to call.

The best way to purge these demon leavings, I have found, is to pull them out of my primordial brain stew and speak them aloud, preferably to someone else, so that another person might be driven crazy as well. Today, I offer you some lyrics, calling upon you to reflect (but not too seriously) upon the damage such a refrain might do rolling around in the consciousness for more than thirty years.

The year: 1962

The artist: Paul Peterson, the actor who played Donna Reed's son, here pretending to sing

The title: "She Can't Find Her Keys"

The situation: A young man has walked his date home and is hoping for a goodnight kiss.

The tune: Mercifully, I'll leave that to your imagination.

The lyrics: She says: "Just a minute please, I can't find my keys." Then he says: "And here's what happens as I'm waitin' for my squeeze. She pulls out lipstick, powder, bubble gum and bobby pins, but she can't find her keys. Find her keys. Curlers, tweezers, cold cream, and candy bars, but she can't find her keys. Find her keys. Nail files, schoolbooks, and autographs of Fabian, she can find with ease, but I'm standing here waitin' for a goodnight kiss, and she can't find her keys."[2]

There are several ways to read this text—almost all of them depressing. Of course, one may think of it, as I am eternally damned to do, whenever I lose my keys. Or we might read it as a commentary on the prefeminist condition: despite the woman's efforts to be prepared for anything she stands outside the locked door of experience, discovering that even though she gathered around her life's accoutrements, she lacks the one instrument of power that she needs. The most hopeful reading, of course, is that she has deliberately misplaced her keys and is waiting for Paul Petersen to slink away into the night. Today, however, I want to use "She Can't Find Her Key" as a metaphor for writing postbellum southern political

2. "She Can't Find Her Keys," Alfred/Gold, sung by Paul Petersen, *Collectable Record Company*, box 35, Narberth, Pa., 19072.

history by incorporating gender and the social construction of race as tools of analysis.

In the past, historians sought the key that would unlock the mystery of southern distinctiveness in the American nation. For Ulrich Bonnell Phillips it was race; for C. Vann Woodward, within the acknowledged surround of white supremacy, it was class; for many of us in this room it has been women and gender.[3] But we might learn a lesson from our keyless "she." Trapped in a futile exercise, she pulls out everything: nothing unlocks that door. Likewise, historians of southern black and white women pile up evidence on the doorstep of southern history, yet studies of southern politics continue to be written as if our work is a heap to be skirted before entering the inner sanctum of southern historiography, the room from which white men called all the shots. There, women and African Americans exist only as objects, never as actors.

After more than twenty years on the doorstep, I think it is time to change our strategy: to give up on finding the key and opt instead to change the lock. We will never find the magic key; henceforth, we

3. There has been a flowering of historical writing on southern women in the past ten years that rests upon an earlier small body of work. Since this paper discusses postbellum politics, I will leave aside foundational work on antebellum southern women, slave and free. Two pathbreaking works on postbellum southern women pointed the field of southern history in new directions: Anne Firor Scott, *The Southern Lady: From Pedestal to Politics, 1830–1930* (Chicago: University of Chicago Press, 1970), and Jacquelyn Dowd Hall, *Revolt against Chivalry: Jessie Daniel Ames and the Women's Campaign against Lynching*, rev. ed. (New York: Columbia University Press, 1993). Of those who followed in the 1980s, some used women's history to turn back to issues of class in the South, including Dolores Janiewski, *Sisterhood Denied: Race, Gender, and Class in a New South Community* (Philadelphia: Temple University Press, 1985); and Jacquelyn Dowd Hall, James L. Leloudis, Robert R. Korstad, Mary Murphy, Lu Ann Jones, and Christopher B. Daly, *Like a Family: The Making of a Southern Cotton Mill World* (Chapel Hill: University of North Carolina Press, 1987). A new wave of scholarship on black women gained strength in the early 1990s, notable for its insistence that black women's history is at the core of southern history. See, for example, Jacqueline Anne Rouse, *Lugenia Burns Hope: Black Southern Reformer* (Athens: University of Georgia Press, 1989); Elsa Barkley Brown, "Womanist Consciousness: Maggie Lena Walker and the Independent Order of Saint Luke," *Signs* 14 (spring 1989): 610–33; Elsa Barkley Brown, "Negotiating and Transforming the Public Sphere: African American Political Life in the Transition from Slavery to Freedom," *Public Culture* 7 (1994): 107–46; Evelyn Brooks Higginbotham, *Righteous Discontent: The Women's Movement in the Black Baptist Church, 1880–1920* (Cambridge: Harvard University Press, 1993); and Tera Hunter, *To 'Joy My Freedom': Southern Black Women's Lives and Labors after the Civil War* (Cambridge: Harvard University Press, 1997).

must insist on a combination lock. All sorts of people live in the house of southern history. It is only by understanding the interconnectedness of their lives that we can understand their politics. Of course, in many subfields, we follow this strategy. We rarely write about southern African Americans without writing about race relations, in other words, without writing about white people and politics. And, in the past decade, we have come to believe that it is difficult to write about southern white women without writing about black women and racial hierarchy. In the future, no one should be able to write about southern white men without writing about gender and race. Yet, even when we cross that threshold—the one beyond which southern white men too have gender and race, we must insist that such work include women and African Americans *acting* in the text to shape those white men's identities. Just as U. B. Phillips knew that there could not be a South without a North, we know that you cannot be man without woman; you cannot be white unless someone else is black.

For all of the ripples that writing on gender and race in the South has made, political history's course continues to flow in a well-worn channel—one excavated by white southern men. Let's trace its familiar contours. After Reconstruction, elite white southern men redeemed the South from an unstable coalition of white Republicans and freedmen; subsequently, they settled intraracial class matters with the defeat of the Populist Party.[4] Sometime before this, or perhaps sometime afterward, depending upon whom you believe, they robbed African Americans of all political rights for more than half a century; thereafter, African Americans figured into politics

---

4. The literature of Reconstruction serves as a good example for centering race as an issue in southern history. Historians write Reconstruction as African American history for several reasons: the very nature of Reconstruction, that is, its biracial concerns; its peculiar historiography as a battleground between white scholars such as those of the Dunning school and W. E. B. Du Bois; and the unusually rich view of African American life left by nonsoutherners on the period. For good examples of Reconstruction history with African Americans in the center, see Leon Litwak, *Been in the Storm So Long: The Aftermath of Slavery* (New York: Alfred A. Knopf, 1988). For an analysis of the contribution of those scholars who pay attention to African American agency during the period, see Harold D. Woodman, "Sequel to Slavery: The New History Views the Postbellum South," *Journal of Southern History* 43 (November 1977): 523–54. Historians are just beginning to put gender into their analyses of Reconstruction. See, for example, Laura Edwards, *"Gendered Strife and Confusion": The Politics of Reconstruction* (Urbana: University of Illinois Press, 1997).

only as rhetorical apparitions brandished at poor whites by demagogues to terrify them into forgoing all self-interest. African Americans coped either by migrating or by lying low in black churches and business districts. Concurrently, a few enlightened, albeit racist, white men seized progressive-era ideology to misshape the social gospel and to introduce stunted reforms. Then the New Deal and World War II pierced the boundaries of regional isolation, offering a glimpse of national values and opportunities that eroded slightly the power base of white demagogues. Ultimately, a courageous generation of charismatic black men with religious training emerged from nowhere in the 1950s and 1960s to draw on international liberation methods to topple white supremacy.

Though overdrawn, this summary serves to magnify the grain of formal political southern history against which we write. W. J. Cash, not Katharine Du Pre Lumpkin, defines the Mind of the South. The Ku Klux Klan, not the National Association of Colored Women's Clubs, represents voluntary associations in the 1920s. The poll tax looms large in accounts of electoral politics, but woman suffrage in the South alters the story only for white women and not at all for white men or African Americans. I could continue, but all of our recovered evidence on the importance of gender and race slides to the margins; the center holds. It is an impassive account of parties, elections, legislation, white male politicians, and realignments, the genre masterfully initiated by V. O. Key. For all of our efforts, we still can't find *our* V. O. Key: the way to rewrite, reperiodize, and reconceptualize southern political history to include all of the political actors, male and female, black and white. Connecting gender and race—seeing southern politics with double vision as black women always have—would tell a tale very different from the one that I just outlined.

The stakes are high: until we write about white supremacy by gendering and racing politics, we simply have no credible explanation of its relatively rapid fall. Just as historians of the Cold War failed utterly to predict the collapse of the communist world, so too did historians of southern politics fail to predict the civil rights movement. Moreover, accounts of southern politics written in the past thirty years portray a system of white supremacy so solid that its demise somehow seems unthinkable even though we know it ended. Cold War and southern historians grossly overestimated the

power of the respective orders of communism and white supremacy. Their work tells us how each flourished; now we need an
explanation of how such totalitarian systems came down in a heap.
Of course, there remain communists in the Soviet Union and racists
in the South. But the system that legitimated them—what Pierre
Bourdieu would call the cultural *doxa*—vanished.[5]

Since it happened so recently, it is understandable that we have
not yet sorted out how history failed to predict the end of the Cold
War, but it is less understandable that we remain without a satisfac-
tory description of the mechanisms of destruction within the white-
supremacist order. This is due partly, I think, to the monumental
catch-up task that historians of the South found thrust upon them
when the civil rights movement opened a floodgate of truth telling
about white supremacy. From the first blow struck by C. Vann
Woodward's 1955 *Strange Career of Jim Crow* to Dan Carter's 1995
Politics of Rage, the task of post-Reconstruction southern political
history has been to explain the origins of the segregated South, and
the disfranchisement of and violence against African American
southerners.[6] In short, the critical task of proving the horror of white
supremacy has been so successful that white men remain on center
stage.

Do not get me wrong. I do not advocate turning away from the
study of white supremacy. In fact, adding gender and race to politics produces a story even more despicable than the one we know.
While historians have sought to document white supremacy, they
have done so for the most part exclusively through the eyes (and
sources) of male white supremacists. Centering white men in our
conceptual, research, and literary strategies distorts the meaning of
politics by privileging the view of the oppressors, thereby minimiz-
ing African American resistance and the importance of gender.

It is time to re-vision the southern political narrative from other
angles to take into account the plethora of sources on African American and women's history, to grapple with the theoretical insight

5. Pierre Bourdieu, *Outline of a Theory of Practice* (London: Cambridge University
Press, 1977), 164.
6. C. Vann Woodward, *The Strange Career of Jim Crow,* 3d ed. (1955; reprint, New
York: Oxford University Press, 1974), and Dan Carter, *The Politics of Rage: George
Wallace, the Origins of the New Conservatism, and the Transformation of American Politics*
(New York: Simon and Schuster, 1995).

that gender and race are socially constructed, and to test new ideas about the junctures of public and private space in political culture. In a little more than a decade, work on southern African Americans has reordered a subfield only recently known as "race relations." By refusing to define race as a "problem," by centering narratives on African American agency, and by making the racial philosophies of their white subjects central to their worldviews, historians of southern African Americans have presented an opening wedge in challenging the orthodoxy of southern political history. They integrated their work into the "master" narrative of the 1960s, but have also gone on to write entirely new narratives using new definitions of politics and social reform. Historians can no longer write of the post-1950 period as if race had little to do with white southern lives or as if the term *southerners* excluded African Americans.[7]

Yet, the categories "southerners" and "African Americans" often signify male southerners and male African Americans, and southern white men still walk about history's pages ungendered. C. Vann Woodward once said of the reappraisal of U. B. Phillips's work: "The re-evaluation of the work of the previous generation is inevitable and essential to the health of each successive generation of historians. . . . The result for . . . scholarship . . . is an uncivil lack of continuity and a rather halting and jerky flow of ideas."[8] Over the

---

7. The literature on African American agency in the post-Reconstruction South built upon the counterhistoriography that historians of Reconstruction began. Major works in this field are Sara Evans, *Personal Politics: The Roots of Women's Liberation in the Civil Rights Movement and the New Left* (Chapel Hill: University of North Carolina Press, 1976); William Chafe, *Civilities and Civil Rights: Greensboro, North Carolina, and the Black Struggle for Equality* (New York: Oxford University Press, 1980); Charles Payne, *I've Got the Light of Freedom: The Organizing Tradition and the Mississippi Struggle* (Berkeley and Los Angeles: University of California Press, 1995); John Dittmer, *Local People: The Struggle for Civil Rights in Mississippi* (Urbana: University of Illinois Press, 1994); Neil R. McMillen, *Dark Journey: Black Mississippians in the Age of Jim Crow* (Urbana: University of Illinois Press, 1989); Nell Irvin Painter, *Exodusters: Black Migration to Kansas after Reconstruction* (New York: Alfred A. Knopf, 1976); Robin D. G. Kelley, *Hammer and Hoe: Alabama Communists during the Great Depression* (Chapel Hill: University of North Carolina Press, 1990); Steven Lawson, *Black Ballots: Voting Rights in the South, 1944–1969* (New York: Columbia University Press, 1976); and Steven Lawson, *Running for Freedom: Civil Rights and Black Politics in America since 1941* (Philadelphia: Temple University Press, 1991).

8. C. Vann Woodward, "'Introduction': *Life and Labor in the Old South,*" reprinted in *Ulrich Bonnell Phillips: A Southern Historian and His Critics,* ed. John David Smith and John C. Inscoe (New York: Greenwood Press, 1990), 111.

past few years, we have watched a halting and jerky flow of ideas trickle out from work on southern women and gender, but those ideas remain dammed up, awaiting the moment when they can break through the continuity of the southern political narrative.

As history becomes comparative, as the study of the state regains favor, and as international concerns replace domestic ones, regional history may face a crisis of irrelevance. Recognizing the interconnectedness of gender and race in southern history can take us in new directions and increase the importance of the field as a whole. The American South affords us a rare opportunity to study a place where gender and race have been central to the creation and maintenance of a political system that countered that of the dominant nation-state.

How might historians of southern women—how might we—finally accomplish our own "uncivil lack of continuity"? In the time remaining, I want to suggest some tools that might change that lock. First, drawing from my own work, *Gender and Jim Crow,* I will relate an incident that has been much chronicled from the white supremacists' view, pointing out how its meaning changes when black women are added as political actors. Then, I will invite you to think about the conventions within our own fields—southern, women's, and African American history—that operate to fragment and to isolate our scholarship. Finally, I will close by suggesting promising frontiers on which some of us are working and to which others of us might migrate.

To illustrate how our understanding of southern politics might change if we interweave gender and racial identities into the story of white men's politics, I will turn to a telescoped view of a single moment: incidents preceding the Wilmington racial massacre of 1898. The action takes place over a few weeks and over a few blocks among people who knew each other, at least on sight. It is the tightness of this vision that allows us to see all of the actors, and it demonstrates a fact that political organizers know well and historians might employ profitably: all politics is local.

It is necessary to spin this analysis from the flimsiest strands of evidence left to us by the most unreliable of sources: whites' complaints of African American women's and girls' street behavior during North Carolina's bombastic 1898 election that culminated in the

Wilmington racial massacre. The white press used these stories during the campaign to demonstrate how African American political success translated into personal ordeals for white women in the hopes that white men would forsake interracial political coalitions between Populists and Republicans. We can use them differently: as indications of young girls' and poor women's politics. In the midst of rhetoric that disparaged them and their families, anonymous black women and girls struck back in the language of the streets.

The white-supremacy campaign itself put black women and interracial sexuality at its center. In August black editor Alexander Manly printed an editorial on interracial liaisons in his newspaper. Manly argued that at least half the time white women lied about being raped. Then he pointed out that white men both raped and seduced *black* women. And he dared to criticize white patriarchy on its own terms: "Poor white men are careless in the manner of protecting their women." Perhaps his worst offense in the eyes of whites was his comment that "the morals of the poor white people are on a par with their colored neighbors of like conditions." By bringing in white women's morals and the rape of black women, Manly committed what the white press called "a dirty defamation," a "sweeping insult to all respectable white women who are poor," and "a great slur."[9]

As Manly insulted white women while defending black women, black women had the capacity to speak for themselves. Since Reconstruction, they had been active in church organizations, Republican Party aid societies, the international Women's Christian Temperance Union, and had recently organized long-standing women's clubs into a national union. This overarching organizational web brought middle-class black women into politics in state, region, and nation even though they could not vote.[10] Black women

9. This account of black women's political agency in Wilmington and the quotations are drawn from Glenda Elizabeth Gilmore, *Gender and Jim Crow: Women and the Politics of White Supremacy in North Carolina, 1896–1920* (Chapel Hill: University of North Carolina Press, 1996), 98–114.

10. The body of work on black women's political and social organizations was so solid and went so unnoticed by those writing southern political history that I began to wonder how the two might look together, a question that resulted in *Gender and Jim Crow*. Scholarship on black women's organizations includes Rosalyn Terborg-Penn, "Afro-Americans in the Struggle for Woman Suffrage" (Ph.D. dissertation, Howard University, 1977); Cynthia Neverdon-Morton, *Afro-American Women of the*

with fewer resources and less time expressed themselves more directly and responded to the local political climate by asserting their rights in daily life. For example, in Wilmington, one white man blamed the enraged passions of the white supremacists there on "the audacious Negro grudge developing against the streetcar conductors because they did not help black women on and off the conveyance as they did white women." A group of white men formed the Wilmington "Minutemen" and vowed to put an end to three things: rising crime, poor policing, and "negro women parad[ing] the streets and insult[ing] men and ladies." Invoking Manassas and Chancellorsville, they armed themselves to the hilt and declared themselves "ready for a little unpleasantness."

Three altercations serve as prototypes of the "parading" and "insulting" that made politics so personal on the streets of North Carolina. For example, in New Bern the daughter of a prominent white family set out on a leisurely stroll down Middle Street. Shortly, she met two black girls, probably teenagers. According to the white press, they were "young and ignorant and therefore impudent [and] had heard of the 'rights' of their race." As the white woman approached, the young girls locked arms and forced her to step off the high sidewalk and into the street as they passed. On another occasion an altercation became more "pointed." One sweltering afternoon, an example of "the loveliest of southern womanhood . . . dressed in white" walked out to get some air on a bridge. As she ambled across, she met a black laundress who thrust "the point of her umbrella into her side." The white woman kept walking, but as she turned to go back across the bridge, she saw the black woman coming toward her again. This time, the laundress poked her harder

South and the Advancement of the Race, 1895–1925 (Knoxville: University of Tennessee Press, 1989); Beverly Guy-Sheftall, *"Daughters of Sorrow": Attitudes toward Black Women, 1880–1920* (New York: Carlson, 1990); Rouse, *Lugenia Burns Hope;* Dorothy Salem, *To Better Our World: Black Women in Organized Reform, 1890–1920* (New York: Carlson, 1990); Evelyn Brooks Higginbotham, *Righteous Discontent: The Women's Movement in the Black Baptist Church, 1880–1920* (Cambridge: Harvard University Press, 1993); and Gerda Lerner, "Community Work of Black Club Women," *Journal of Negro History* 59 (1974): 158–67. Newer works that also put black women's history into other historical conversations include Anne Firor Scott, *Natural Allies: Women's Associations in American History* (Urbana: University of Illinois Press), and Elizabeth Lasch-Quinn, *Black Neighbors: Race and the Limits of Reform in the American Settlement House Movement, 1890–1945* (Chapel Hill: University of North Carolina Press, 1993).

with the umbrella and shouted, "Oh, you think you are fine!" Finally, an incident in Wilmington involved both sidewalks and um-
brellas. When several white women encountered a black woman
deliberately standing in their way on the sidewalk, one of them
"caught hold of the negress to shove her aside to prevent the intended collision, and the negress viciously attacked her with an umbrella." A black male bystander shouted encouragement: "That's
right; damn it, give it to her."

What is going on here? There are at least three possibilities. First,
the stories may be completely or partially fabricated, urban legends
on the order of poisoned wells, to arouse white male voters. Second,
the white women, inspired by the election campaign, could have
been reporting incidents that heretofore had been commonplace but
unreported. Third, and the case I would make, the sidewalk altercations represent a departure from normal interaction; the stories are
at least partially true, and the laughter, poking, and physical isolation of white women by black women reflect political actions that
produced a terrible response from white men.

Black and white women had met each other on the streets day in
and day out since emancipation. What was different now? For one
thing, the white women probably *were* putting on airs, since the
white-supremacy campaign daily depicted them as virginal trea-
sures under assault from "Negro domination" in politics. The black
women understood these "airs" to result from political winds. At the
same time the black women *were* more militant. In the months before the election of 1898, white editors slandered African American
women openly and reacted to their increased visibility by insulting
them whenever possible. Moreover, white politicians concocted a
bogus rape epidemic that implied that the Populist/Democratic
split had given black men the chance to exercise not only political
equality but also sexual equality. In the streets, black women championed their right to hold political opinions and their husbands'
right to vote, but they also literally struck back at a white-supremacy
campaign that made the political personal by encouraging white
women to treat them shabbily in public and by defaming black
women's morality and their husbands' characters. Two days after
the election, Wilmington's white men struck back as well, spraying
the city's streets with a Gatling gun, body searching black women
on the sidewalks, and murdering black men where they stood.

Examining the politics of the 1890s exclusively through the eyes of white men does more than neglect the African American experience, it distorts the white-supremacy campaign's meaning by ignoring its context. What white men did and thought is important because they held the preponderance of power and used it so brutally. White men knew, however, what historians are discovering: that they did not act with impunity in a lily-white male world; rather, they reacted strategically in a racially and sexually mixed location. Moreover, the victories they won were not ordained or complete but began as precariously balanced compromises that papered over deep fissures in southern life. In the end, white men may have constituted only half of the story. White women's support was crucial, as were the sophisticated political ideology, the complicated class and gender dynamics, and the rising resistance of African Americans.

Acknowledging agency to everyone involved yields a more nuanced view of southern politics and reveals that white power was protean, the master of a thousand subtle and not-so-subtle disguises. By including all of the actors, we learn that North Carolina's "white-supremacy campaign" responded to black power even as it capitalized on black weakness and that young Jim Crow hatched and perched in a more precariously balanced nest than we might have imagined. Moreover, these stories move the debate from white Populists' racial ideology—something we may never discern—to the opportunity that the rift in the Democratic Party created for African Americans at the polls and on the streets. Finally, the incidents point toward highly developed political cultures. Much has been made, and rightly so, of elite white women's "indirect influence" in politics prior to the Nineteenth Amendment. But what of elite black women's indirect influence? And how did poor women, black and white, conceive of and act out their politics?

Having proposed my own uncivil, halting, and jerky reinterpretation of a particular political moment in southern history, I turn now to the ideological constructions that operate in our profession to prevent gendered and raced explanations from impinging on the larger story, those that allow postbellum southern political history to flow as a mighty undammed river of white-male supremacy. There are at least four assumptions at work.

The first is not peculiar to southern history; rather, it is common in history at large: the assumption that women's and African American history are contribution history. Most of us grasped this insight in our second class meeting in women's history, but we must apply it to southern history. Anne Scott's pioneering study of southern women began as a history of the Progressive Movement in the South, and ended as a history of women in politics in the South. She literally "stumbled" over women as progressive leaders in her research. Unfortunately, other historians keep stumbling over Anne Scott, rather than actually grappling with her redefinition of Progressivism. Historians then, Scott reports, asked if her "insistence upon paying so much attention to women [wasn't] simply a form of female chauvinism." To which she replied, "my concern is less to do historical justice to women than to add to our understanding of what has been social reality." Scott understood then the limitations of contributing history; unfortunately, subsequent works on Progressivism in the South continue to do an injustice to the "social reality" of the period. They fail to grapple with the meaning of the striking insight that women took the lead in southern Progressivism, failing to ask how that reshapes what we know about the dynamics of the period. Instead, chronicler after chronicler congratulates himself when he includes a chapter or scatters in paragraphs on women's contributions into a narrative that chronicles a male-driven Progressive Movement.[11]

The second conceptual restraint is more subtle. In our late-twentieth-century understanding of the limitations of gender solidarity we have become critical of an earlier tendency to find sisterhood among black and white southern women in unlikely places. Yet, I would urge us not to forget that sometimes sisterhood *was* powerful, that southern women, black and white, could be feminists, and that on many occasions southern women sharply questioned and even subverted the gender-based version of white supremacy. Elizabeth Fox-Genovese has criticized historians for

---

11. Scott, *The Southern Lady*, ix–xii. William Link's *The Paradox of Southern Progressivism, 1880–1930* (Chapel Hill: University of North Carolina Press, 1992) comes closest to including women as progressive-era leaders, but I would go even further than Link does to argue that, in the South, even more than in the North, women took the lead in progressivism because many white male politicians, to serve their primary goal of dividing the races in order to keep power, kept social services to a minimum.

giving in to the "temptation to view southern women" (and here I think she is speaking of southern *white* women) "as committed, if frequently secret, social critics." Certainly, Fox-Genovese has argued eloquently that most upper-class antebellum southern white women subscribed to the basic tenets of their culture.[12] Yet, in the postbellum South some white women did become critics, and highly vocal ones at that, despite the strictures they faced. In writing about those exceptions, we must always acknowledge that such women went against the grain of the social system in which they lived. That is the point. In studying those who promoted social change, we are not misrepresenting southern society; we are seeing it through the eyes of its critics. It would be impossible to understand how the South changed over time without recovering the ideologies of middle-class southern white women who came to criticize the powerful society that produced them, even though it sometimes did them in.

Moreover, to assess completely the subversion that sisterhood wrought, we must remember that southern women were also black and working class. We are just beginning to recover black women's political activism, thanks in large part to the theoretical and research standards that Elsa Barkley Brown's work has set for the rest of us. New portraits of poor and working-class black and white women by Jacquelyn Hall, Laura Edwards, Martha Hodes, and Victoria Bynum remind us that class complicated gender norms and produced space for resistance that shaped legal and customary constraints.[13]

12. Elizabeth Fox-Genovese, "Steward of Their Culture," in *Stepping Out of the Shadows: Alabama Women, 1819–1990,* ed. Mary Martha Thomas (Tuscaloosa: University of Alabama Press, 1995), 11; and Fox-Genovese, *Within the Plantation Household: Black and White Women of the Old South* (Chapel Hill: University of North Carolina Press, 1988).

13. Elsa Barkley Brown, "Uncle Ned's Children: Negotiating Community and Freedom in Post-Emancipation Richmond, Virginia" (Ph.D. dissertation, Kent State University, 1994); Brown, "Negotiating the Public Sphere"; Jacquelyn Dowd Hall, "O. Delight Smith's Progressive Era: Labor, Feminism, and Reform in the Urban South—Atlanta, Georgia, 1907–1915," in *Visible Women: New Essays on American Activism,* ed. Nancy Hewitt and Suzanne Lebsock (Urbana: University of Illinois Press, 1993), 166–98; Edwards, *"Gendered Strife and Confusion";* Martha Hodes, *White Women, Black Men: Illicit Sex in the Nineteenth-Century South* (New Haven: Yale University Press, 1997); Victoria E. Bynum, *Unruly Women: The Politics of Social and Sexual Control in the Old South* (Chapel Hill: University of North Carolina Press, 1992).

Third, historians of the South have only begrudgingly allowed that gender might be socially constructed and hence changeable over time; even now many are not convinced that gender applies to guys. For the most part, treatments of southern masculinity have become snagged on the ahistorical dichotomy of the honorable antebellum white man and the touchy southern yeoman. It is as if white southern manhood has been cryogenically preserved, cloaked either in an antebellum suit fashioned from honor or topped off by a coonskin cap. W. J. Cash contributed disastrously to this legend. But while Cash imagined only two types of southern men, ironically, he ignored the man *he* was: an urban, middle-class reporter harnessed to wage labor by a New South rag; a commuter, living with his mama in nearby Shelby. He finished *The Mind of the South* not propped under a magnolia tree or gazing out at some boll-weevil-mangled cotton field, but in a most unlikely spot: holed up in an apartment in Charlotte, North Carolina, creating his romantic dreams of the dead southern men he could never become.[14]

Historians, often fascinated by *The Mind of the South,* have enlivened Cash's fantasy by extending Bertram Wyatt-Brown's and Steven Stowe's work on honor among antebellum elite men into the postbellum period, as if such a slippery and historically contingent concept could exist over decades, yea over generations, and throughout classes to define white manhood. Ted Ownby's work on rural evangelical white men represents the other point of this horned dilemma.[15] Yet, in examining a record of the good ol' boy

---

14. Bruce Clayton, *W. J. Cash, a Life* (Baton Rouge: Louisiana State University Press, 1991), 79–116. The Cash cult continues, but his detractors increase. See Paul D. Escott, ed., *W. J. Cash and the Minds of the South* (Baton Rouge: Louisiana State University Press, 1992).

15. Bertram Wyatt-Brown, *Southern Honor: Ethics and Behavior in the Old South* (New York: Oxford University Press, 1982); Steven M. Stowe, *Intimacy and Power in the Old South: Ritual in the Lives of the Planters* (Baltimore: Johns Hopkins University Press, 1987); Ted Ownby, *Subduing Satan: Religion, Recreation, and Manhood in the Rural South, 1865–1920* (Chapel Hill: University of North Carolina Press, 1990). Wyatt-Brown argued that aristocratic white southerners were so far above slavery that the institution and black people had virtually nothing to do with the construction of honor. Recently, Kenneth Greenberg has turned Wyatt-Brown's thesis on its head. Greenberg argues that slavery had everything to do with the construction of southern honor, since anything associated with slavery served as the polar opposite of the honorable act or course and hence drove definitions of honor (*Honor and Slavery: Lies, Duels, Noses, Masks, Dressing as a Woman, Gifts, Strangers, Humanitarianism,*

when we have no idea of his more numerous and urbane contemporaries, we find ourselves once again in a position to define
southern manhood by its extremes—dueling or huntin', racing thor-
oughbreds or stalkin' possums—forced to choose one's phallic symbols between golf clubs or shotguns.

As important as work on honor and hell-raisin' is, we cannot
leave male gender constructions there. Centering the study of
southern manhood on such binary formulations tells us little about
what manhood meant to the urban, middle-class white men who
built the New South, less about how politicians deployed gender as
a rhetorical tool, and nothing at all about how black men both formulated definitions of manliness and sought to circumvent white
men's formulation of *man* as *white*. Three new examples drawn from
the belly of the beast itself, South Carolina, push the connections between manhood and politics and tantalize us with their daring.
Stephanie McCurry's *Masters of Small Worlds* analyzes the connections between the household, patriarchy, and slaveholding in the
antebellum period. Steven Kantrowitz's forthcoming study will
begin to redefine the importance of gender to the rise of white supremacy. Kantrowitz's title, *The Reconstruction of White Supremacy:
Violence, Politics, and Manhood in Ben Tillman's World,* is filled with
promise. Bryant Simon's recent article in the *Journal of Southern History,* "The Appeal of Cole Blease of South Carolina: Race, Class, and
Sex in the New South," moves into the twentieth century, demon-
strating how Blease manipulated poor white men's concepts of
manhood to guarantee his own election, while pouring balm on the
injuries of class.[16] Through a gendered analysis of Blease, Simon
proposes a new answer to an old question: how could poor southern white men continually vote against their own class interests?
Soon, it seems, we may recapture the historical antecedents to those
Citadel boys.

---

*Death, Slave Rebellions, the Proslavery Argument, Baseball, Hunting, and Gambling in the
Old South* [Princeton: Princeton University Press, 1996]).

16. Stephanie McCurry, *Masters of Small Worlds: Yeoman Households, Gender Relations, and the Political Culture of the Antebellum South Carolina Low Country* (New
York: Oxford University Press, 1995); Bryant Simon, "Appeal of Cole Blease," *Journal of Southern History* 62 (February 1996): 57.

The fourth disciplinary limitation is our Balkanization of history. The subfields of the discipline—African American history, women's history, social history, political history—are drawn by and for historians. Analyses that separate these subfields misrepresent the way people actually lived their lives. This practice has particularly dire consequences for the study of the postbellum South, where politics was not just an electoral pursuit, but instead a tenacious legal and extralegal system that constantly struggled to redefine democracy, an effort that required policing the thoughts and actions of all southerners. Writing about a place in which politics dictated where to get a drink of water or where to direct one's gaze while walking down the street requires a powerful reconceptualization of the public sphere.

The scholars who have most shaped my thinking about the reconstruction of the political in southern history are Robin D. G. Kelley, Elsa Barkley Brown, Nell Painter, and Jane Dailey. Expanding the site of the political to places where African Americans practiced resistance, these scholars are beginning to build a cultural anthropology of the postbellum South. We have completely recovered the electoral manifestations of an antidemocratic cultural and social system mandated by politics, but we fail to understand the warp and woof of that system. Pierre Bourdieu argues, "Every established order tends to produce . . . the naturalization of its own arbitrariness. Of all the mechanisms tending to produce this effect, the most important and best concealed is undoubtedly the dialectic of the objective chances and the agents' aspirations, out of which arises the *sense of limits*, commonly called the *sense of reality*."[17] The white supremacists sought to naturalize racial oppression and deliberately, through custom and law, to create a new sense of limits after Reconstruction. They succeeded in making those limits reality for

17. Robin D. G. Kelley, " 'We Are Not What We Seem': Rethinking Black Working-Class Opposition in the Jim Crow South," *Journal of American History* 80 (June 1993): 75–112; Brown, "Negotiating the Public Sphere"; Nell Irvin Painter, " 'Social Equality,' Miscegenation, and the Maintenance of Power," in *The Evolution of Southern Culture*, ed. Numan B. Bartley (Athens: University of Georgia Press, 1988), 47–67; Jane Dailey, "Deference and Violence in the Postbellum South: Manners and Massacres in Danville, Virginia," *Journal of Southern History* 63 (August 1997): 553–90; Bourdieu, *Outline of a Theory*, 164.

all but a few whites—a subject about which we must learn more—
but this new work gives us reason to believe that they failed in their
attempt to do so for blacks.

Finally, to underscore the politics of daily life and to understand
our own immersion in it, I want to end my call for a re-envisioning
of postbellum southern political history by noting the one perspective that historians of the South tend to avoid at all costs: their own.
In other words, I want to close by tasting the forbidden fruit: autho-
rial self-positioning. Rather than accepting the dictum of dispassion
in our writing, rather than approaching our topic from the neutral (I
might say neutered) and professionalized ground most historians
were ordered to occupy in graduate school, I think that we should
write passionately about southern history, recognizing that all of us
have a stake in the story we are telling. Self-referential writing has
gained acceptance in anthropology, cultural studies, and literary
criticism, but historians of the South eschew it, perhaps because
their subject matter is so tortured, perhaps because their training is
so conservative. Yet, we do not have to look to literary criticism or
feminist theory for a model; as is often the case in the writing of
southern history, C. Vann Woodward was there first, in *Thinking
Back*.[18]

Taking self-position seriously in your writing matters because
"ontogeny recapitulates phylogeny." That was the first sentence of
my comparative anatomy textbook in college; the one that almost
sent me running to drop/add. But I learned quickly what it meant.
The developmental cycle of an embryo (ontogeny) replicates the
evolutionary cycle of the species (phylogeny). For white southerners and for all African Americans, the development of the white-
supremacist system that we study at a scholarly remove is inscribed
on generations of our families, and it is, often in ways we do not
know, inscribed on our selves.

Black writers have left moving accounts of coming to color
consciousness. W. E. B. Du Bois's lesson came subtly, in a genteel

---

18. C. Vann Woodward, *Thinking Back: The Perils of Writing History* (Baton Rouge:
Louisiana State University Press, 1986). Another wonderful example of using the
historian's craft and autobiography is Melton A. McLaurin, *Separate Pasts: Growing
Up White in the Segregated South* (Athens: University of Georgia Press, 1987).

manner, when a new white girl at school refused his visiting card: "Then it dawned upon me with a certain suddenness that I was different from the others; or like, mayhap, in heart and life, and longing, but shut out from their world by a vast veil." White southerners must have come to racial consciousness in order for segregation to work, but among the few accounts we have is Katharine Du Pre Lumpkin's. Her lesson came wildly, in a barbaric manner, when she found her father beating the black cook with a stick: "The inevitable had happened, and what is bound to come to a Southern child chanced to come to me this way. Thereafter, I was fully aware of myself as a white and of Negroes as Negroes. Thenceforth, I began to be self-conscious about the many signs and symbols of my race position that had been battering against my consciousness since virtual infancy."[19]

In genteel and in barbaric ways we learned "race." Our genealogical and personal ontogeny recapitulates our phylogeny. It is in us; we are in it. Growing up in North Carolina as a white girl in the 1950s, I lived white supremacists' fiction as reality. The subsequent separation of self from lies consumed much of my postadolescent, post–civil rights movement life, as I painfully peeled away a tissue of falsehoods and cut through many connections to my upbringing in segregation. After that, I believed no truth and took no evidence at face value. Fiction in the archives? What else?

It is precisely because my personal ontogeny recapitulated the South's political phylogeny that I argue that, in the Jim Crow South, politics were personal and self-identity always shaped political expression. When I came upon the sidewalk incidents I described, I *knew* them. I could visualize them as clearly as if I had been there. Then I remembered, I *had* been there. In the aftermath of the initial sit-ins at Woolworth's in Greensboro, my hometown, everyone remained tense. Protests moved to the cafeteria, people gathered in the streets, and all of us, even an eleven-year-old white girl, felt exquisitely, self-consciously political and important. Walking down a city street one day with my grandmother, I noticed two young black

19. W. E. B. Du Bois, *Souls of Black Folk*, quoted in David Levering Lewis, *W. E. B. Du Bois: Biography of a Race* (New York: Henry Holt, 1993), 33; Katharine Du Pre Lumpkin, *The Making of a Southerner* (1946; reprint, Athens: University of Georgia Press, 1991), 132–33.

girls—adolescents—approaching arm in arm, taking up slightly more than half of the sidewalk. Well! I was ready for them. They wouldn't integrate my sidewalk like they had integrated my lunch counter. I was white, I was raised a segregationist, I knew my place, and I knew theirs. So I stuck my nose in the air, looked at a spot two inches over their heads, and walked straight toward them, giving no quarter. That meant that the swift kick one of them gave me came as a complete surprise. Before I could pick myself up, they were gone. But they were not the only ones gone. My grandmother—the woman who had schooled me in the prerogatives of whiteness—ran like a turkey.

I remember the moment as a gear shifting in the universe. At once I knew I had been wrong to taunt them. Wrong to assume that they would take my airs and not react. But most important I heard a fire bell in the night: the day would soon come—indeed, might have arrived—when I could not get away with feigning racial superiority anymore, even if I wanted to. Whiteness lost a lot of value for me that day.

In much the same way, my genealogical ontogeny—my family history—was contrived to underscore our purity. My grandmother never mentioned her Cherokee ancestry and clung fiercely to her whiteness. But then so did her great-great-great-grandmother, the Cherokee. When Andrew Jackson's soldiers burst into her house to force her and her children to march on the Trail of Tears, she sank to the floor, wrapped herself around her white husband's leg, and screamed, "I'm not Cherokee, I'm Black Irish." On the spot, she constructed a fictional white identity, and, confounded, the soldiers left her; thus, I am a seventh-generation "white" North Carolinian, not a sixth-generation Cherokee Oklahoman. On the other side of my family, the middle name of choice for men is Manly, borrowed from our illustrious ancestor, Governor Manly. Imagine my surprise when I learned that the governor also lent his name to his other family: the black Manlys. Alexander Manly, it seems, is my distant cousin. Does this mean that my family's racial identity was Native American and black? No, in a society where race is a made-up thing, we simply pruned the darker branches off the family tree. We segregated our very selves.

Why does revealing the fiction of purity in southern white families matter to the project of writing southern political history? Family, personal experience, and sex matter to politics because such personal perspectives enable us to see the larger system that created them. Michel Foucault understood sexuality as central to the exercise of power, a "linchpin" for an infinite variety of power configurations. Friedrich Engels saw gender in much the same way, suggesting that the inequity and hierarchy in society had roots in the family. Foucault and Engels tell us that the lessons that one learns about "otherness" and power are taught early, in the home. Feminists in the 1960s realized this and began to theorize societal changes rippling out from changes in the family unit.[20]

While we have indications that patriarchy is dying a lingering death, we are reminded constantly that racism is not; rather, it is thriving. We attack it in the marketplace through affirmative action, yet it rears its head and swallows the remedy whole. We desegregate the schools, only to relocate the focal point of racial strife in society at large to the educational system. We pay lip service to equal housing, yet residential segregation triumphs. For the past half century, we have attacked the mutant growth of racism everywhere except at its root: in the family. It is in the family that one learns gender, and it is there that one learns race, first by forming primary bonds with other family members and then by forming a separate self-identity. We cannot eliminate racism by continuing to attack its manifestations, by continuing to try to assuage, after the fact, "fear of the stranger." If friends and lovers, husbands and wives, and children crossed racial lines, there would be no need for any of the other remedies for discrimination. White southerners knew this in the nineteenth century, and they made miscegenation laws the cornerstone of white supremacy.

As Stephanie McCurry's work has demonstrated for the antebellum period, the patriarchal structure of the family created both a sense of limits and empowerment for white yeomen. Martha Hodes reminds us that love crossed the color line, acting on politics and lawmaking, which in turn acted on love. Laura Edwards's *"Gendered Strife and Confusion": The Politics of Reconstruction* argues that

---

20. Michel Foucault, *History of Sexuality*, 3 vols. (New York: Pantheon Books, 1978–1986); Frederick Engels, chapter 2, *The Origin of the Family, Private Property, and the State*, reprinted in Miriam Schneir, ed., *Feminism: The Essential Historical Writings* (New York: Vintage Books, 1972), 189–204.

the patriarchal family structure shaped Reconstruction by furnishing ways to circumvent true equality and by holding out manhood as an ultimately empty promise for black men. Jacquelyn Hall's work on Katharine Du Pre Lumpkin examines how home mediated race, class, and gender consciousness for Katharine as one family's politics cohered and broke with southern politics.[21] These historians remind us that white southern men fought a long and successful fight to keep the family patriarchal and mono-racial. That fight was as political as casting a ballot.

Such work helps us question the cultural *doxa* that continues to define our own "sense of limits," our own "sense of reality." White supremacy depended and depends upon understanding the southern family as racial—as black or as white—a conception as artificial as patriarchy. We must look within ourselves as well as within the archives, questioning our own conceptions of love, power, and family. All of us, white and black, were wounded and bent by white supremacy. We must think hard about how it stunted our lives and our imaginations. As we begin to drive southern history in new directions, we must remember that "objects in the mirror are closer than they appear." Our pasts—personal and collective—are present within us. Our key we hold in our hands.

21. McCurry, *Masters of Small Worlds*; Edwards, *"Gendered Strife and Confusion"*; Jacquelyn Dowd Hall, *Writing Memory: Katharine Du Pre Lumpkin and the Refashioning of Southern Identity* (forthcoming).

Tokens of Affection

The First Three Women Presidents of the Southern Historical Association

C A R O L   B L E S E R

June 1997
Fourth Southern Conference on Women's History
Charleston, South Carolina

In 1990 an exhibit of portrait miniatures appeared at the Metropolitan Museum of Art, the National Museum of American Art, and the Art Institute of Chicago. The exhibition's accompanying publication was titled "Tokens of Affection." In America and Europe personal images of friends and loved ones were frequently recorded in diminutive paintings called portrait miniatures. In America the brief history of portrait-miniature painting spans approximately the century between 1750 and 1850. As highly prized as full-size portraits in oil, these tiny paintings were painted on ivory and presented in elaborate cases or frames or mounted in brooches, lockets, bracelets, necklaces, rings, and watch fobs. The charm of a small, delicate portrait, the fascination of its precise detail, continues even today to attract the connoisseur, but by 1850 its day was over, supplanted or suppressed by the ubiquitous photographic image.

For as long as I can remember, I have been interested in the art of miniature portraiture. Much like the talented miniaturists I admire, I am also drawn to the letters written by Maria Bryan of Mount Zion, Georgia. Like them, the tools and materials she used in her art were portable and small—a goose-quill pen and plain paper. The results, however, were quite extraordinary. Much like the finding

145

of a painting on ivory in a nineteenth-century locket, Maria successfully captured in her antebellum correspondence a vanished civilization in miniature exactness. Thus, when the pleasure was given
to me of editing and publishing Maria Bryan's remarkable letters, it
seemed most appropriate to title the book *Tokens of Affection: The
Letters of a Planter's Daughter.*[1]

Maria began her correspondence to her sister in 1824, when she
was sixteen years old and her sister, Julia, then twenty-one years
old, had just married and moved away from their home at Mount
Zion to Augusta, Georgia. For more than two decades from the mid-
1820s to the mid-1840s, Maria produced a picture of the life of a
slaveholding family living on a middling-size plantation in Mount
Zion, a small southern frontier community, seventy-five miles from
Augusta. In Maria's letters we encounter a woman of remarkable
education and taste. She recounts to Julia in Augusta, at that time
the third largest city in Georgia, the myriad of details of life in rural
Georgia.

Nothing much is known of Maria's childhood, except that she
grew up in a piously Presbyterian household, comfortably fixed,
and surrounded, in general, by people of education and taste. It is
assumed that Maria attended Nathan Beman's Mount Zion Academy, one of the most celebrated educational institutions in the early
history of Georgia. Despite her extraordinary, rich classical education, the lot of a nineteenth-century educated southern woman was
not rich in opportunities. Her options were to marry and confine
herself to domesticity, or to remain single and care for aging parents. Maria's letters reveal some resentment at the fact that she was
expected to always defer to the men in her life—her father, uncle,
brothers, brother-in-law, suitors, and male friends, few of whom
may have been her equal in matters of the mind. On one occasion,
when helping to grade end-of-term papers for Professor Beman, albeit on the quiet, a male student discovered that a female had cor-
rected his composition, which so "riled him," wrote Maria, "that he
tore his oration into a thousand pieces and positively refused to
speak it."[2]

1. Carol K. Bleser, *Tokens of Affection* (Athens: University of Georgia Press, 1996).
2. Ibid., 79.

Maria, a very attractive dark-haired beauty, as her portrait miniatures show, had enough social charm and conversational ability to
collect several marriage proposals. She married twice, but bore no
children. Maria, although childless, seemingly was astute in the
raising of Julia's many children, who frequently visited her at Mount
Zion for extended visits of a year or more. As suddenly as Maria's
letters started in March 1824, they abruptly ended at her death on
January 15, 1844, at the age of thirty-six. Julia, pregnant at the time
with her eighth and final child, named her daughter, born in March
of that year, Maria Bryan Cumming, in memory of her dearly
beloved sister.

The memory of Maria's life, which could have been only a faded
name on a moldy tombstone in the Mount Zion cemetery, endures
because Julia, following the unexpected death of Maria, put her sister's letters away in neat bundles, sentimental tokens of affection of
her sister's brief life.

Unlike Maria and almost all women throughout most of recorded
history our choices today are seemingly unlimited. The Southern
Historical Association's pioneering women presidents were remembered at a session on November 13, 1980, at the tenth-anniversary
meeting of the Southern Association for Women Historians. I had
the honor as president of the SAWH to preside over that session
held during the forty-sixth annual meeting of the Southern Historical Association. At the Atlanta meeting the three women remembered were Ella Lonn, SHA president in 1946, Kathryn Abby Hanna
in 1953, and Mary Elizabeth Massey in 1972. All three women have
now been deceased for more than twenty years. They are also remembered today, as is Maria Bryan, primarily for their writings.
What follows is primarily drawn from that session held in 1980 and
already published in *Southern Studies*.[3]

A year after Ella Lonn retired from a twenty-seven-year teaching
career in the history department at Goucher College in 1945, she
became the first woman president of the SHA. Her appointment to
the Goucher faculty in 1918 came through a teachers' agency
in Chicago. She was actively seeking another academic position,

---

3. Carol K. Bleser, ed., "The Three Women Presidents of the Southern Historical
Association: Ella Lonn, Kathryn Abby Hanna, and Mary Elizabeth Massey," *Southern Studies* (summer 1981): 101–21.

according to the agent's letter, but "I incline to think you could get her as there is not much chance for a woman at Grinnell." Ella Lonn was more than pleased to receive an appointment in the department of history at Goucher (she had been reduced at Grinnell to teaching German only), but she was not happy with the status offered her— an instructorship with an annual salary of fourteen hundred dollars. She was a woman of forty, with more than eleven years of teaching experience, five at the college level and with the rank of assistant professor. Her first book, *Reconstruction in Louisiana after 1868*, had been published that spring by C. P. Putnam's Sons.[4]

Ella Lonn's professional reputation rests upon six books: *Reconstruction in Louisiana, Desertion during the Civil War* (published in 1928), *Salt as a Factor in the Confederacy* (in 1933), *Foreigners in the Confederacy* (in 1940), *The Colonial Agents of the Southern Colonies* (in 1945), and *Foreigners in the Union Army and Navy* (in 1951), written six years after her retirement, when she was approaching seventy-three.

Ella Lonn's appointment as the first woman president of the SHA came when she was sixty-eight years old. We are told gender played no role either for or against her. We are also told that the leading male leaders of the SHA accepted and valued her for her scholarship. In the words of one, she was "a studious, objective, no-nonsense scholar." Leaders of the SHA who knew her remember Ella Lonn as gentle in nature, modest, somewhat retiring, feminine but not feminist, with "no cause to promote such as woman's rights."[5]

Ella Lonn's commitment to the recognition of women was not apparent in her scholarly work except peripherally, but as an active member of the AAUP and the American Association of University Women, she made outstanding attempts at advancing the careers of women professionals. She was a keynote speaker at the annual conference of the AAUW in 1923, a delegate to the International Federation of University Women in Norway in 1924, and from 1925 to 1929 [from 1924 to 1928?] chairman of the standing Committee on

4. Faculty Records, Office of the President, Goucher College. See Bleser, "Three Women Presidents," 105.

5. Thomas D. Clark to LaWanda Cox, April 1, 1980; E. Merton Coulter to LaWanda Cox, April 4, 1980. See Bleser, "Three Women Presidents," 105, 104.

Recognition, a critically important and arduous responsibility that she once termed "truly a labor of love." At that time the AAUP had appointed a Committee W, composed of seven women and four men, on the Status of Women in College and University Faculties, which made a preliminary report in 1921 but delayed another until three years later. Meanwhile, in her 1923 address Ella Lonn succinctly summarized their preliminary report and then presented the results of a supplementary inquiry that she had made single-handedly. She had analyzed seventy university catalogs, sent out 202 questionnaires, and both raised and answered the critical question that the AAUP committee did not face even in its second report: "What are we, as individuals, and as an association, able to do to improve this situation [the unsatisfactory status of women]?"[6]

Her answer included financial support to women for advanced graduate training and publication of their scholarly articles, a standing committee "to watch the situation closely," and an exchange of faculty members between men's and women's colleges. Other remedies that she tried to implement in passing upon the applications of colleges and universities for recognition by the AAUW were "a fair proportion" of faculty appointments for women "not merely [those] in the instructors' rank to do the drudgery," impartial promotion, a reasonable burden of teaching hours, justice in regard to salary, opportunity for administrative posts other than that of "a glorified chaperon or house-mother," and representation on policy-making committees and on boards of trustees! Although in the 1923 address she cautioned women against "undue impatience and ill-timed efforts," she concluded by answering those men "who may think that we women are needlessly impatient." She did so with the words of a young woman who was leaving the university at which she had taught for several years "without other reward for hard work than more hard work: 'I am leaving. I am so sick of seeing the honors all go to the men on every occasion that I cannot endure it longer.' "[7]

6. She was a member of the AAUP from 1922 until her death in 1962, and from 1936 through 1947 chaired the association's committee on admission of members. Marie Welebir, Administrative Secretary, AAUP, to LaWanda Cox, May 15, 1980. See Bleser, "Three Women Presidents," 107.

7. Ella Lonn, "Academic Status of Women" and "The Work of Recognition." Her questionnaires had revealed a widespread perception that women were not as

The second pioneering woman president of the SHA, Kathryn Trimmer Abby, was born November 5, 1895, into the family of a prominent Chicago attorney. Upon finishing her preparatory work at the Stickney School, she was admitted to Northwestern University, where she received a B.A. in 1917. With interludes of teaching at Lenox Hall in Saint Louis and Hood College in Maryland, she received an M.A. and, finally, a Ph.D. in 1926 from Northwestern. Kathryn Abby was invited to be on the program of the American Historical Association within eighteen months after receiving her Ph.D. She read a paper titled "Spanish Projects for the Re-occupation of the Floridas during the American Revolution," and in the summary of the proceedings it was stated that there was no question of her scholarship—the sources were detailed and impressive. The young scholar was in distinguished company at this session of the association, which included J. Franklin Jameson, Tyler Dennett, Roy F. Nichols, Frederick A. Shannon, and Avery Craven.

Kathryn Abby's dissertation dealing with the Floridas indicated the area that was to hold her major intellectual and academic interest. When she heard of a faculty opening at Florida State College for Women (later to become Florida State University) she moved rapidly to secure the position for herself. With the unqualified support of her professors at Northwestern and the recommendations of the administrators at Hood College, she went to Tallahassee in 1926. Her rise through academic ranks was rapid; an associate professor in 1926, she became a full professor in 1927, and chairman of the Department of History, Geography, and Political Science in 1930.[8]

Professor Abby's first important publication was *Florida, Land of Change*, published by the University of North Carolina Press in

---

productive as research scholars as were men. Her response was " 'Not yet.' We women must produce more research of a uniformly high caliber on *worthwhile* subjects," undaunted by the knowledge that "the rewards of scholarship are greater for a man than for a woman, as even good work seldom wins promotion or new calls for us." She conceded that women more than men yielded "to the temptation of dissipating our energies with social, civic, and philanthropic work" ("Academic Status of Women," 10).

Her reference to administrative opportunities other than that of "a glorified chaperon" probably reflects dissatisfaction with her first postdoctoral appointment, at Fargo College, North Dakota, where she not only taught history but was dean of women for one year, 1911–1912. See Bleser, "Three Women Presidents," 107–8.

8. Bleser, "Three Women Presidents," 110–12.

1941. It was the first comprehensive history of the state. Isaac J. Cox of Northwestern in his review of the volume said: "This book is a result of a double adoption. Dr. Abby, even before taking up teaching of history, had adopted Florida as her specialty; and the historical guild and its associates in her adopted state almost as quickly adopted her. . . . This book is a personal and professional milestone for the author and the region she represents."[9]

In the year of the publication of *Florida, Land of Change*, Abby, at the age of forty-six, married Alfred Jackson Hanna, professor of history at Rollins College and later its vice president. Following her marriage and following the convention of the time, Mrs. Hanna in 1941 resigned her tenured senior-faculty position. Thereafter, she and her husband collaborated in research and writing. This team was now to branch out beyond the boundaries of Florida by beginning research in Central and South Americas. In the summer of 1946 they worked in the archives and libraries of Mexico, Colombia, and Venezuela. Their major interest was French intervention in Mexico, but an early by-product of the research was the volume titled *Confederate Exiles in Venezuela*. The major work of the Hannas was *Napoleon III and Mexico: American Triumph over Monarchy*, published by the University of North Carolina Press in 1971. This volume was the result of more than a quarter century of work in the archives in South and Central Americas, Canada, England, France, and the United States. Mrs. Hanna was not to see these years of research brought to culmination, as she died in 1967.

The indexes of such professional publications as the *Journal of Southern History*, the *Mississippi Valley Historical Review*, the *Hispanic American Historical Review*, and the *Florida Historical Quarterly* show countless entries under the name of this remarkable woman. She wrote articles, reviewed books, had books reviewed, chaired meetings, read papers, made comments, served on committees, and held numerous offices.

Perhaps it was in the Southern Historical Association that Hanna was most active. Together with Kathleen Bruce of Hollins College and Dorothy Dodd of Florida State Library, she was present at the

---

9. Isaac J. Cox, *Journal of Southern History* 8 (1942): 106–8. See Bleser, "Three Women Presidents," 112.

organizational meeting of the SHA on November 2, 1934. She steadily progressed by way of membership on the executive council, committee on program, committee on membership, committee on nominations, board of editors, the vice presidency, and finally, in 1953, the presidency. The minutes of that year read: "The annual business was conducted with commendable, though unhurried, dispatch." Her presidential address, "The Role of the South in French Intervention in Mexico," was described as a scholarly study of an exciting episode, skillfully told.[10]

Nineteen years elapsed before another woman became president of the SHA. The third woman to serve as president, Mary Elizabeth Massey, was born in Morrilton, Arkansas, in 1915. She graduated from Hendrix College in Conway, Arkansas, in 1937, earned her M.A. and Ph.D. from Chapel Hill and moved to Rock Hill, South Carolina, to become an associate professor of history at Winthrop College in 1950. She remained there until her death at the age of fifty-nine in 1974. Perceived by Winthrop students as demanding, informed, and witty, Massey was named four times as outstanding teacher by senior classes. Hendrix College named her an outstanding alumna in 1967, and Winthrop chose her Distinguished Professor in 1965. Although Massey published ten articles and numerous book reviews, her scholarly reputation rests on her three books—*Ersatz in the Confederacy* (published in 1952), *Refugee Life in the Confederacy* (in 1964), and *Bonnet Brigades: American Women in the Civil War* (in 1966)—and on her 1972 SHA presidential address, "The Making of a Feminist."[11]

Refugee Life is, perhaps, her best book. It is certainly the most thoroughly researched. The bibliography cites 131 manuscript collections, and the text and footnotes reveal that numerous letters and unpublished diaries were used. Ten summers of research went into *Refugee Life,* and the time was well spent. The book contains many

10. *Journal of Southern History* 30 (1954): 3ff. See Bleser, "Three Women Presidents," 114.

11. Mary Elizabeth Massey, *Ersatz in the Confederacy* (Columbia: University of South Carolina Press, 1952); Massey, *Refugee Life in the Confederacy* (Baton Rouge: Louisiana State University Press, 1964); Massey, *Bonnet Brigades: American Women in the Civil War* (New York: Knopf, 1966); Massey, "The Making of a Feminist," *Journal of Southern History* 39 (February 1973): 3–22. See Bleser, "Three Women Presidents," 116.

examples and some analysis of southern women, their behavior, and their roles. Husbands and wives disagreed over whether or not wives and children should remain at home during the Civil War, or flee. Women refugees struggled to provide for their families amid galloping inflation and dwindling incomes, worked in government in Richmond, and attempted to continue their social activities as well as to make and sell jellies, hats, and soap. Some even wrote for newspapers and magazines.

The increasing opportunities that the war opened for women, suggested in *Refugee Life,* becomes a major theme in *Bonnet Brigades,* Massey's last book. Prewar northern and southern women had become increasingly "restless," Massey wrote, as men went off to war. Women, as a result, "appeared to be breaking out in all directions at once."[12] Women worked as teachers, nurses, in factories, as clerks, and in a host of other occupations and professions. They participated in draft riots, gave advice to governments on military tactics, served as spies for both sides, went on strike for higher wages, raised large amounts of money for various causes, ran farms and plantations, and campaigned for emancipation and black rights. Like Massey's other books *Bonnet Brigades* is packed with brief, enticing case studies. Although her books discuss general trends, Mary Elizabeth Massey was always happiest when she could write about individuals, and the vignettes of persons and their individual experiences make engaging reading. The author's discussion of southern women of invention is, not surprisingly, fuller than her account of northern ones.

When the opportunity came for Professor Massey to deliver her presidential address at the meeting of the Southern Historical Association in 1972, she chose an individual woman as her topic. She selected Ella Gertrude Clanton Thomas (who lived from 1834 to 1907), whose diary she had planned to edit, an enterprise never completed because of Dr. Massey's death in 1974. Thomas, a prewar Georgia belle, survived the catastrophes of the Confederacy and continual disappointments with her flawed and financially incompetent husband. She bore ten children and raised five, and still found time to keep a detailed journal, to write numerous magazine

12. Massey, *Bonnet Brigades,* 3, 174. See Bleser, "Three Women Presidents," 117.

and newspaper articles, to become an active member of organizations such as the WCTU, to work for women's education and many other causes, and eventually to become an active supporter of suffrage. Ella Gertrude Clanton Thomas's life, as Massey clearly demonstrated, showed the gradual emergence of a southern woman from domesticity through women's organizations to feminism. Her extraordinary journal, *The Secret Eye,* would be skillfully edited by a descendent of Thomas, Virginia Ingraham Burr, with a long introduction by Nell Irvin Painter and published by the University of North Carolina Press in 1990.

The presidency of the Southern Historical Association gave Mary Elizabeth Massey immense personal satisfaction. As one might expect from a student of Fletcher Green and one who had first met Ben Wall in the stacks of the library at Chapel Hill when both were graduate students, Mary Elizabeth Massey was devoted to the SHA. The association was the place where she saw her many friends, a group that included most of the major figures of southern history. Her correspondence, which is available to scholars at the Winthrop College Library, reveals warm associations with many, including Bell Wiley, Fletcher Green, Rembert Patrick, Alan Nevins, Issac Copeland, Edwin Miles, Howard Beale, George Tindall, T. Harry Williams, A. Elizabeth Taylor, Mattie Russell, David Donald, John Hope Franklin, and, of course, Ben Wall. She worked her way up in the SHA from chairman of the membership committee to chairman of the program committee, to chairman of the nominating committee, vice president, and, at last, president. In all the many offices she held, she worked hard and effectively to forward the association's work, by performing tasks that she found a bit tiresome at times, but always did well. In 1971 she wrote Dewey Grantham: "I think you must have held up better when you were a high mogul in the SHA than I am doing. All that can be said for me is that I'm muddling through and probably driving Ben nuts. He's a big help to me and I'm trying to adjust to his methods of working but as yet haven't figured out what his methods are."[13]

The early 1970s had seen the growth of the women's movement nationally and within the Southern Historical Association. Upon as-

---

13. Massey to Grantham, October 25, 1971, Mary Elizabeth Massey Papers, Winthrop College, South Carolina. See Bleser, "Three Women Presidents," 119.

suming the presidency in 1971, Mary Elizabeth Massey told the *Houston Post:* "The records seem to indicate that women have gotten fewer promotions and lower salaries, but that hasn't been my experience at all. I knew I was getting into a field predominated by men when I chose history and I brought the matter up with the man who directed my graduate work at the University of North Carolina. I just told him bluntly that 'I've heard you don't welcome women.' 'It's not that we don't welcome them,' he told me. 'It's just that we don't do anything for them.' "[14]

Massey had strong views on the course women's history should take as a field of study. In 1961 in response to a congressman who wanted to know which southern women should be honored during the Civil War centennial, Massey urged that "little-known women" should be recognized. "Mary Boykin Chesnut of South Carolina will probably be suggested by someone, but I have carefully read her diary many times and cannot find anything she did that merits recognition. . . . I recommended that any woman be recognized only for what she did and not for the name she carried." Mary Elizabeth Massey qualified *somewhat* her views on the treatment of women in the profession when she wrote in 1972 that although she opposed hiring quotas, "when a man and a woman with equal credentials are being considered for a position, and there is an imbalance within the department, an effort should be made to remedy said imbalance."[15] It has been suggested to me in private conversations that the title of her talk, "The Making of a Feminist," may have been more personal than originally thought.

A devoted teacher, a successful and recognized scholar and author, a witty and valued colleague, and a sympathetic commentator on the women's movement and women's history, Mary Elizabeth Massey deserves to be read and remembered as a founder of women's history in the South. Professor Massey died in 1974 just when the unparalleled explosion of interest occurred in southern women's history.

14. *Houston Post*, November 19, 1971, p. 5B. See Bleser, "Three Women Presidents," 119.

15. Massey to Fred Schwengel, September 21, 1961, Massey Papers; Massey to Nancy N. Barker, June 20, 1972, Massey Papers. See Bleser, "Three Women Presidents," 120.

The lives of the first three women presidents of the SHA reveal noteworthy similarities. All three pioneers taught in women's colleges, were outstanding and meticulous scholars who did their research primarily on the South, and included in their publications subjects in social history that were then outré—women, foreigners, deserters, and exiles—but that since then have drawn the attention of hundreds of historians, so much so that we now have extremely well-attended conferences devoted essentially to the study of women's history. These three women's commitment to the profession seemed all-consuming. Ella Lonn and Mary Elizabeth Massey never married, and Kathryn Abby married historian Alfred Jackson Hanna in her forty-sixth year. Despite their noteworthy public achievements, it appears that these three pioneering women shared the same fate as that of portrait miniatures—tokens of affection, passed over, superseded, and almost forgotten by the SHA. That certainly was my impression when the *Journal of Southern History* chose not to publish the article that came out of that SAWH session in 1980, the article on the first three women presidents of the SHA: Ella Lonn, Kathryn Abby Hanna, and Mary Elizabeth Massey, prepared by Profs. LaWanda Cox, Blanche Clark Weaver, and Frederick Heath. That article, with my introduction, appeared in 1981 in *Southern Studies*. I vowed at the time that if I ever became president of the SHA I would read that article as my presidential address, thereby guaranteeing its publication in the journal!

Seventeen years following Mary Elizabeth Massey's presidency of the SHA, Prof. Anne Scott of Duke University became the fourth woman president of the SHA, almost two decades after the publication in 1970 of her pathbreaking book, *The Southern Lady*. What has followed in the historical profession from Professor Scott's breakthrough book is more than twenty-five years of prodigious research and writing in southern women's history. This fourth conference sponsored by the SAWH and held in 1997 in Charleston, South Carolina, showcases this latest work. A great debt of gratitude is owed by all of us to Prof. Anne Scott.

Although I might truly say to all the scholars of women's history, "Go forth, the world is your oyster," I might issue the following warning. Despite the incredible acceleration that we have observed in the last two decades in the writing of women's history, the road ahead is still very long in improving the professional status of those who write this history. Let us consider Clemson University, where I am employed as a historian, not as unique, but as representative of the institutions we live and work with. If we look at the top forty-one people in the administrative and academic ranks of the university, only one of them is a woman. If we look at the sixty-one departmental chairmen, only three are women. If we look at the nearly five hundred senior academic positions at Clemson, less that 10 percent are held by women after forty-two years of coeducation.[16] Clemson University, let me assure you, is a fair representation of the larger world of which it is a part. In general, this is the status of academic women today.

The challenge to us all is to complete the journey that was begun more than fifty years ago by the pioneering women presidents of the SHA.

16. The President's Commission on the Status of Women at Clemson University Report, fall 1996.

"A Stronger Soul within a Finer Frame"
Writing a Literary History of Black Women

DARLENE CLARK HINE

November 1997
Atlanta, Georgia

> Into the furnace let me go alone;
> Stay you without in terror of the heat.
> I will go naked in—for thus 'tis sweet-
> Into the weird depths of the hottest zone.
> I will not quiver in the frailest bone,
> You will not note a flicker of defeat;
> My heart shall tremble not its fate to meet,
> My mouth give utterance to any moan.
> The yawning oven spits forth fiery spears;
> Red aspish tongues shout wordlessly my name.
> Desire destroys, consumes my mortal fears,
> Transforming me into a shape of flame.
> I will come out, back to your world of tears,
> A stronger soul within a finer frame.

The words of the poet Claude McKay in his poem "Baptism," "a stronger soul within a finer frame," refer to the refining of soul and body that takes place when a person undergoes a baptism of fire, and I do want to conjure that image, so appropriate to Black women. I want to evoke those women the depths of whose souls and inner lives have been long hidden from view. Their experiences have been and are shaped by the social relations in which they find themselves, yet each individual or collective soul, I suspect, is stronger because it is protected by a self-created frame—the public self—that absorbs the shock of societal bombardment.

158

In borrowing McKay's metaphor, however, I am also changing its meaning. We historians too often think of our work as the *substance* of history, the "frame" in the sense of body or structure. In fact, however, what we do when we think, research, and write about the past is to create a frame in another very different sense. We gather our insights, biases, and ordering concepts, and we knock them together to form an encompassing border around one piece of the picture that has been painted by the lived experience of the past. As a result, a historian's frame is a way of choosing what will constitute the history. The historical frame consists of the analytical constructs of gender, class, race, sexuality, and location, or geography. But these analytical constructs are neither static nor exhaustive, and historians need to craft a finer frame, a better-defined, more refined understanding of the institutional matrix or matrices with which we surround Black women's history.

Those of us committed to the centering of Black women's history need now to define our frame. By this I mean that we need to critique our consumption of theories that were constructed with Black women as the "other." We must find new ways to take that which is not ours and make it our own. Black women's experiences with gender differ from those of white women and Black men. Thus, refining the frame, as a process, necessarily involves creating and expanding our methodologies and finding forms through which we can more clearly depict the "soul" with all its complexity. We must expand the multiple subjectivities of Black women, a task that is possible only by taking into account Black men and white women and men.

Some of the most exciting and dynamic work being done today in the academy focuses attention on the social history of Black women. I believe that examining some of this work leads us to a "frame" that could enhance our understanding of Black Women's Studies, which both permeates and erodes boundaries between traditional disparate disciplines. Constructing this frame involves attention to a specific type of intellectual work, namely, the autobiographical writings of Black women both outside and within the academy. These writers occupy, in a sense, the frontier sites of public discourse concerning certain private-life issues and social policies that are important to the reconstruction of Black community and family and to revisions of self.

Black women's studies scholarship transgresses history, literature, and the social science disciplines of sociology, psychology, and an-thropology. My present reading and teaching project surveys ap-proximately forty intriguing and provocative autobiographies written by contemporary celebrity and lesser-known ordinary Black women, as well as scholars working in the field of Black Women's Studies. To be sure, it is daunting to keep on top of the emerging his-torical and academic scholarship, even given the relatively small numbers of Black women professors. But the tremendous outpour-ing of autobiographical writings presents a more complex set of challenges, not the least of which concerns the difficulty of find-ing the volumes that they fill. Many are privately published, with limited print runs and strictly regional distribution. Yet, autobiog-raphy, surely the most ancient genre of literature and memory, pos-sesses profound implications for the creation of new courses and conversations in Black women's history, women's history, and African American studies.

To date, there have been two waves of scholarship in the emerg-ing field of Black Women's Studies. The first wave highlighted and protested the exclusion, neglect, and invisibility of Black women. The second wave goes further, insisting on the urgent need to trans-form humanistic scholarship in the academy. In other words, follow-ing the first wave, we determined that inclusion is not enough. Scholarship of the second wave recognizes that it is no longer suffi-cient to add Black women and stir, leaving the structure and over-arching power of the master narrative intact. Fully to recognize Black women as historical subjects with discernible historical agency is to raise new questions, introduce imaginative methodologies, un-earth new and reassess old sources, and inspire and enrich our ana-lytical arsenal of concept and theory.

The first wave of Black women's studies was overwhelmingly concerned with reclamation, in both tone and content. Because Black women shared membership in two groups considered mar-ginal in the race and gender hierarchy in America, it was easy for them to slip through the cracks. It was assumed that whatever was known and said about white women and about Black men applied equally to Black women. This reasoning denied the need for, or value in, specific and distinct study of Black women in their own right. Even more invidious was the argument that Black women's absence from historical texts and established literary canons proved that they had made no contributions to the development and evolution of American society that warranted sustained investigation. The conclusion was an incorrect, but logical, one, and it led to the further conclusion that the invisibility of Black women, whether self-imposed or not, was justified. All the women were white, and all the Blacks were men, as the book *But Some of Us Are Brave: Black Women's Studies* attests.[1]

The initial challenge was to identify Black women. Who are they? What did they write, create, produce, think, feel, know, and contribute? What do they look like or sound like or consume? What are their gestures, words, values and beliefs, concerns and roles? The reclamation work that answered some of the questions spanned a temporal continuum that extends from the 1972 publication of Gerda Lerner's *Black Women in White America: A Documentary History* to the release in 1993 of the two-volume *Black Women in America: An Historical Encyclopedia,* which I coedited with Elsa Barkley Brown and Rosalyn Terborg-Penn.[2]

Between 1970 and 1993 several works appeared that laid the foundation of Black women's studies in history and in literary criticism. Time and space permits the noting of only a few select titles that appeared on reading lists in the first courses and seminars. Sharon Harley and Rosalyn Terborg-Penn edited the first collection of historical articles, *The Afro-American Woman: Struggles and Images* (published in 1978). A decade later, two of the contributors—Evelyn Brooks Higginbotham and Cynthia Neverdon-Morton—would publish major volumes in Black women's history. In the introduction to the 1997 edition of their volume, Harley and Terborg-Penn reflected on their initial motivation and perspective. "We took a Black nationalist feminist position, revealing how racism stood as the primary obstacle in the way of African American achievements. . . . In addition, the contributors viewed Black women's lives and activities from a perspective inside the African American communities

---

1. Gloria T. Hull, Patricia Bell Scott, and Barbara Smith, eds., *All the Women Are White, All the Blacks Are Men, but Some of Us Are Brave: Black Women's Studies* (Old Westbury, N.Y.: Feminist Press, 1982).

2. Gerda Lerner, *Black Women in White America: A Documentary History* (New York: Random House, 1972); Darlene Clark Hine, Rosalyn Terborg-Penn, Elsa Barkley Brown, *Black Women in America: An Historical Encyclopedia* (Brooklyn: Carlson Publishing, 1993; paperback ed., Bloomington: Indiana University Press, 1996).

looking out, rather than as outsiders looking in."[3] Terborg-Penn's own work on Black women and the suffrage movement is to be published by Indiana University Press by the fall of 1998.

Deborah Gray White's *Ar'n't I a Woman?* explored the history of Black women in the plantation South and thus signaled the emergence of monographic Black women's history. Wilma King's *Stolen Childhood* looked at the lives of enslaved children. Brenda Stevenson's *Life in Black and White* advanced comparative analysis, and Elizabeth Clark-Lewis's *Living In, Living Out* studied the agency of domestic workers in Washington, D.C. Elsa Barkley Brown's illuminating articles and theoretical essays have shed new light on the political activities of Black women during Reconstruction, while Rosalyn Terborg-Penn's forthcoming *African American Women and the Struggle for the Vote, 1850–1920* reshapes our thinking about the suffrage movement. Stephanie Shaw's *What a Woman Ought to Be and to Do* investigated Black professional women at the end of the nineteenth century, while Evelyn Brooks Higginbotham chronicled the *Righteous Discontent* of Black women and religion. Tera Hunter's *To 'Joy My Freedom'* and Cynthia Neverdon-Morton's *African American Women of the South and the Advancement of the Race* explored southern Black women's lives, work culture, and resistance in the New South. Jacqueline Rouse's *Lugenia Burns Hope*, Nell Irvin Painter's *Sojourner Truth*, Barbara Ransby's forthcoming *Ella Baker*, and Paula Giddings's *Ida B. Wells-Barnett* enrich the biographic study of Black women leaders.[4] We also eagerly anticipate forth-

3. Evelyn Brooks Higginbotham, *Righteous Discontent: The Women's Movement in the Black Baptist Church, 1880–1920* (Cambridge: Harvard University Press, 1993); Cynthia Neverdon-Morton, *Afro-American Women of the South and the Advancement of the Race, 1895–1925* (Knoxville: University of Tennessee Press, 1989); Sharon Harley and Rosalyn Terborg-Penn, eds., *The Afro-American Woman: Struggles and Images* (Baltimore: Black Classic Press, 1997), iii.

4. Deborah Gray White, *Ar'n't I a Woman?: Female Slaves in the Plantation South* (New York: Norton, 1985); Wilma King, *Stolen Childhood: Slave Youth in Nineteenth-Century America* (Bloomington: Indiana University Press, 1995); Brenda Stevenson, *Life in Black and White: Family and Community in the Slave South* (New York: Oxford University Press, 1996); Elizabeth Clark-Lewis, *Living In, Living Out: African American Domestics in Washington, D.C., 1910–1940* (Washington: Smithsonian Institution Press, 1994); Stephanie Shaw, *What a Woman Ought to Be and to Do: Black Professional Women Workers during the Jim Crow Era* (Chicago: University of Chicago Press, 1996); Tera W. Hunter, *To 'Joy My Freedom': Southern Black Women's Lives and Labors after the Civil War* (Cambridge: Harvard University Press, 1997); Jacqueline Anne Rouse, *Lugenia Burns Hope: Black Southern Reformer* (Athens: University of Georgia Press,

coming studies by Valinda Littlefield, Thavolia Glymph, Wanda Hendricks, and Bernice Barrett.

Two outstanding recent contributions to the study of Black women deserve special note: Glenda Gilmore's *Gender and Jim Crow* and Leslie Schwalm's *A Hard Fight for We*. They join the important contributions that others have made, including those by Susan Smith, Christie Farnham, Jacqueline Jones, Kathleen Berkeley, Catherine Clinton, Elizabeth Fox-Genovese, and Dolores Janiewski to name only a few.[5]

Any act of reclamation is an implicit indictment and rejection of the status quo, of prevailing nations concerning the nature of history and the worth of the reclaiming group as historical agents. There are writers and scholars who have argued that Black women were included in women's history and in Black history and therefore did not need a separate and distinct history. Many continue to insist that history should be a chronicle of universal ideas and illustrious thinkers, or that it should recount only great accomplishments, and concentrate on the lives and careers of major political and military leaders, captains of industry, and moguls of business and finance. But Black women know that most American history as taught and written today concerns, at best, only about 20 percent of the total population. As historian Gerda Lerner has astutely

———
1989); Nell Painter, *Sojourner Truth: A Life, a Symbol* (New York: W. W. Norton, 1996); Paula Giddings, *Ida B. Wells-Barnett* (forthcoming).

5. Glenda Elizabeth Gilmore, *Gender and Jim Crow: Women and the Politics of White Supremacy in North Carolina, 1896–1920* (Chapel Hill: University of North Carolina Press, 1996); Leslie Schwalm, *A Hard Fight for We: Women's Transition from Slavery to Freedom in South Carolina* (Champaign and Urbana: University of Illinois Press, 1997); Susan Smith, *Sick and Tired of Being Sick and Tired: Black Women's Health and Activism in America, 1890–1950* (Philadelphia: University of Pennsylvania Press, 1995); Christie Farnham, *Women of the American South: A Multicultural Reader* (New York: New York University Press, 1997); Jacqueline Jones, *Labor of Love, Labor of Sorrow: Black Women, Work, and the Family from Slavery to the Present* (New York: Basic Books, 1985); Kathleen Berkeley, *Like a Plague of Locusts from an Antebellum Town to a New South City, Memphis, Tennessee, 1850–1880* (New York: Garland Publishing, 1991); Catherine Clinton and Michele Gillespie, eds., *The Devil's Lane: Sex and Race in the Early South* (New York: Oxford University Press, 1997); Elizabeth Fox-Genovese, *Within the Plantation Household: Black and White Women of the Old South* (Chapel Hill: University of North Carolina Press, 1988); Dolores E. Janiewski, *Sisterhood Denied: Race, Gender, and Class in a New South Community* (Philadelphia: Temple University Press, 1985).

observed, "the truth is that history, as written and perceived up to now, is the history of a minority, who may well turn out to be 'the subgroup.' "[6]

Ultimately, the study of Black women should transform what we now know, or think we know, about every aspect of Black and female experiences in America. Such transformative work—the second wave of Black women's studies—is already well under way. We now know, for example, that an examination of Black women's quest for the franchise sheds new and rather uncomplimentary light on the women's suffrage movement, not only in the Midwest but also throughout the country. The scholarship of historian Rosalyn Terborg-Penn demonstrates the extent to which white suffragists eschewed sisterhood and embraced racism as part of a bargain for support from southerners. When Black women, as was the case in Chicago, acquired the ballot, we now know, thanks to the research of Wanda Hendricks, that the Black community, for the first time in a northern area, was able to elect a Black representative, Oscar De Priest. Their political work changed the shape and complexion of Black urban politics.

Similarly, Gloria Hull's study of the treatment of Black women poets during the Harlem Renaissance reveals the depth of Black male chauvinism. Yet, when the work of creative Black women is accorded serious analysis it challenges previously held notions of the substance and significance of the Harlem Renaissance. The recent works of Hazel Carby, Mary Helen Washington, Deborah McDowell, and Henry Louis Gates Jr. are striking examples of the impact that the discovery and reclamation of nineteenth- and twentieth-century Black women's literary texts are having on traditional canons in that guild.

Black women's studies scholarship is now becoming more sophisticated and theoretical. Deserving special note because of their analytical brilliance and sophistication, for example, are the articles and books written by historians, such as Elsa Barkley Brown's " 'What Has Happened Here': The Politics of Difference in Women's History and Feminist Politics" and Evelyn Brooks Higginbotham's "African-American Women's History and the Metalanguage

6. Gerda Lerner, *The Majority Finds Its Past: Placing Women in History* (New York: Oxford University Press, 1979), 158.

of Race," both anthologized in *"We Specialize in the Wholly Impossible": A Reader in Black Women's History,* edited by Darlene Clark Hine, Wilma King, and Linda Reed, published in 1995.

Even with all this tremendously important work being carried on, however, many topics still cry out for further investigation. In particular, we know all too little about the inner lives of Black women. We as yet still need to develop theoretical concepts that will permit the exploration of their lives outside of the family, their club work, and religious settings. We need to move beyond the more traditional and predictable themes in Black women's history to probe the texture of intragender relationships and the development of internal resistance strategies. Fully to comprehend the wide range of Black women's unique historical experiences and their creative productions at the intersection of race, class, and gender necessitates focused attention on the constancy of their struggle to be free and fully human. We must now simultaneously participate in, and become familiar with, several discourses and probe deeper into the cultural context of a variety of written expression.

One of the discourses that promises to yield even greater insight into these inner worlds and increase our understanding of the social constructions of race, gender, and class is the discourse of Black women's autobiography. African American women have been writing autobiographies since the 1861 publication of Harriet Jacobs's *Incidents in the Life of a Slave Girl.* Today, the many forms of autobiography—memoirs, essays, notes, diaries, advice, and self-help—constitute one of the most important genres in Black writing. And the autobiographical voices of Black women also include many unwritten forms, such as dance, quilting, and expression embodied in actions.[7]

7. Harriet A. Jacobs, *Incidents in the Life of a Slave Girl: Written by Herself,* ed. L. Maria Child and Jean Fagan Yellin (Cambridge: Harvard University Press, 1987); Maria W. Stewart, *America's First Black Woman Political Writer: Essays and Speeches,* ed. Marilyn Richardson (Bloomington: Indiana University Press, 1987); Ida B. Wells Barnett, *Crusade for Justice: The Autobiography of Ida B. Wells* (Chicago: University of Chicago Press, 1970); Anna Julia Cooper, *A Voice from the South* (New York: Oxford University Press, 1988), facsimile of the 1892 edition, with an introduction by Mary Helen Washington; Frances Ellen Watkins Harper and Maryemma Graham, *Complete Poems of Frances E. W. Harper* (New York: Oxford University Press, 1988); Katherine Dunham, *Dances of Haiti* (Los Angeles: Center for Afro-American Studies, University of California, Los Angeles, 1983).

It was during my recent experience of collaborating with Kathleen Thompson, a white, nonacademic feminist author, to write *A Shining Thread of Hope: The History of Black Women in America* that I first really understood how little insight the structural dynamics of Black women's lives reveal into their internal realities.[8] Thus, we focused on and used another set of analytical categories consisting of culture, consciousness, and community to illuminate deeper themes and meanings of what it is to be a Black woman in America.

It became very clear to us as we worked that the frame had to be rendered less distracting and dominant, while the soul had to command our attention. How else would the collaborative work of a Black woman academic and a white woman feminist resonate to a broader nonacademic audience? Over the months we searched for Black women's voices and found many underused autobiographical writings and expressive cultural productions: music, art, dance, theater, photography, oral stories, movies, and fragments. In order to decipher more complexly the content and context of Black women's culture, consciousness, and community building we had to expand existing arsenals of research methods and sources. Autobiographical writings, memoirs, fragments, and narratives of Black women proved to be enormously useful self-representations, although fraught with monumental problems. These written texts along with their expressive cultural productions when taken together, however, gave us the prism we needed to weld their testimony together with the scholarly work so recently generated by academicians. I, in the process, came to appreciate the magnificent range of Black women's voices.[9]

Having said all of this I would like to return to the title of this presentation, "A Stronger Soul within a Finer Frame." I believe that the

8. Darlene Clark Hine and Kathleen Thompson, *Shining Thread of Hope* (New York: Broadway Books, 1998).

9. *The more traditional expressions of voice* are through performance in the public domain, either in writing or in verbal expression. Lucy Terry and Phillis Wheatley (who lived from around 1753 to 1784) introduced Black women's written voice during the American Revolutionary era. In a letter from 1774, Phillis Wheatley wrote, "In Every human Breast, God has implanted a Principle, which we call Love of Freedom." Wheatley started both the tradition of Black women writing and Black American literature when she published, in 1773, a book of poetry: *Poems on Various Subjects, Religious and Moral.*

power constructs that Black women's historians have used and that compose the frame of our work need refinement. The scholarship produced over the past two decades has perhaps told us more about the frame than we know about the picture it encapsulates or borders. The soul in the metaphor is Black women's consciousness and culture. Our challenge remains how to arrive at a better understanding of Black women's experiences as they maneuvered within specific institutional barriers, thereby allowing us to grasp their individual consciousnesses and their shared culture in their relations with each other and with their families, community, and broader society. A "stronger soul" suggests that Black women's textured history will not gel until we recognize its many expressive features and fully appreciate the layered and nuanced social relations in which Black women are engaged. The soul forces of Black women, their culture and consciousness and relations to their communities and families, interact with the dominant social constructs in ways that often obscure the women themselves and cloud the power relations, the internal realities and actual lived experiences that we aim to study and illuminate.

Can we articulate a portrait of Black women before their history was framed? Frames can do a lot of things to a picture, either enhance, distort, diminish, or distract attention from it. We have assumed that an analysis of gender, that is to say, differences and similarities between Black men and Black women and their relations to each other, will help us to get a sharper and more inclusive history of Black people. In our use of gender as a frame of analysis we did anticipate that our subject, that is, Black women, might, perhaps, migrate out of the picture, somewhat overpowered by the power construct. The steps we took to hold down our migrating subjects layered the frame of gender with constructions of race, class, sexuality, and location. That seemed like the right thing to do.

Black women and white women in the South occupy much the same, though not identical, space in relation to white patriarchy and capital. But even beyond a shared location it is important to underscore that Black women's and white women's different histories do not emerge separately. Their female worlds of desire and relative subordination are firmly intertwined around and by the rope of white male privilege and power.

In an earlier essay I urged scholars of Black women's history to look more closely at white women's history as a way of understanding Black women's experiences with oppression and the development of a culture of resistance that on the surface seemed to privilege race above gender. To advance the study of Black women and white women within a common discourse necessarily involves acknowledgment and dissection of white women's complicity in and perpetration of oppression and exploitation of Black women throughout the course of our history.

The aim is not to refresh the pain of victims and survivors or to raise degrees of guilt in the blameful. Rather, the goal is to refine the frame so that the picture or presence of Black women will emerge with greater clarity. This piercing of the power constructs that keep us from seeing Black women is made even more difficult because of Black women's own use of the veil of dissemblance to protect their souls from view. While it was an important survival strategy for most of this century and before, dissemblance has, perhaps, outlived its usefulness. The strategy has to be one of making the world see Black women and hear their myriad voices.

Today, the frame that upholds Black women's history can either encase it, constrain it, restrict it, enlarge it, deepen it, or complement it. A "finer" frame would be one less rigid and static, and therefore more capable of accommodating diverse elements of analysis, including not only such variables as sexuality and location but also others as they are identified. We need a more flexible and complex analytical framework within which to examine Black women's lives. As we now know, when marginalized groups empower themselves and weaken any of the traditional constructs, others, or combinations of others, emerge to sustain the original power relations. We must not become sanguine about all that has been accomplished in the past two decades in the history of Black women's history. Indeed, there is now the urgency to take the hazardous step of disseminating Black women's history to the broader public, nonacademic audience if it is to become institutionalized and at the same time do its transformative work. Historians must speak to the people whose lives they study. But, more important, they must listen to the voices.

There are many strategies that Black women have employed to construct and articulate a distinct and effective *voice*, one that would not only tell their truths but also advance their political agenda of liberation from the oppression that they have experienced. Black women's voice is forever shifting and transforming itself, and not all Black women use voice in the same way. I have identified six forms of Black women's voice. They are: (1) embodied voice—gestures, dance, sports; (2) oral voice—public speaking, vocal music; (3) written voice—all genres, autobiographies, poetry, prose, novels, short stories, essays, history; (4) creative voice—paintings, sculptures, photography; (5) adornment voice—cosmetics, hair, fashion; and (6) dynamic voice—reproduction, resistance, work.

The *embodied voice* begins on the simplest, most everyday level. In the form of gesture, it consists of hands on hips, rolling eyes, pursed lips, frowning or smiling face, shrug of the shoulders, tilt of the head, a waving of the hand, or a steady stare. All of these gestures convey meaning that the astute observer may readily decipher. For Black women, they have often been shaped by the urgency of expression under conditions of silence and danger. They form an underground communication that is "heard" by the mainstream culture only on occasion, under carefully chosen and controlled conditions, and are important tools in Black women's culture of dissemblance. In secure company, however, they can also embody exuberance, humor, and joy.

When gestures are stylized, codified, and performed with music, they forge a powerful voice that blends dance with sound. Evidences of the dance of Black women in America go back to the seventeenth century. In the words of Kariamu Welshe Asante, "The first, silent generation of dancers laid the foundation by maintaining a connection and intimacy with the earth, dancing under a full moon, remembering the power of ritual in Africa, marking moments for remembrance. They danced whenever there was birth, marriage or death; and even if they wished for the latter, dance helped to affirm life. . . ." The highest expression of embodied voice is exemplified in the twentieth century in the lives and performances of Katherine Dunham and Judith Jamison.

The *oral voice* begins with conversation, with metaphor and trope, with understatement and elaboration. The legendary storytelling abilities of Lucy Terry Prince (who lived from around 1730 to 1821) of Deerfield, Massachusetts, fall into this category, although we know of them only by reputation. This voice is also strongly expressed in vocal music, from the juba rhymers of the eighteenth century to the blues singers of the twenties and beyond. And it is evident in the powerful public speaking of such Black women as Maria Stewart, who gave lectures to mixed groups of men and women in Boston in the early 1830s, and Sojourner Truth, who combined speech and song in the cause of abolition.

For our purposes, the *written voice* includes all genres of writing: autobiographies, poetry, prose, novels, short stories, essays, and history. Lucy Terry Prince and Phillis Wheatley (who lived from around 1753 to 1784) introduced Black women's written voice during the American Revolutionary era. Of Prince's work we have only one poem, written when she was still a teenager. Wheatley, however, started the tradition of Black women writing, and Black American literature itself, when she published a book of poetry titled *Poems on Various Subjects, Religious and Moral,* which was published in 1773.[10] It was the first book by an African American and the second by a woman to be published in the United States. In a 1774 letter Phillis Wheatley wrote, "In Every human Breast, God has implanted a Principle, which we call Love of Freedom," and many of her poems reveal this same spirit.[11]

Harriet Jacobs, Harriet Wilson, Frances Ellen Watkins Harper, and Mary Ann Shadd Cary continued to articulate the voice with notable creative interventions during the antebellum era.[12] In 1859, Harriet E. Wilson (who was born around 1827, but her date of death is unknown) became the first Black person to publish a novel in the United States. Henry Louis Gates Jr. in commenting on her book, *Our Nig,* wrote: "she revised significantly what was known as the white woman's novel and thereby made the form her own. By this act of formal revision, she *created* the Black woman's novel, not merely because she was the first Black woman to write a novel in English, but because she *invented* her own plot structure through which to narrate the saga of her orphaned mulatto heroine. In this

10. Phillis Wheatley, *The Collected Works of Phillis Wheatley* (New York: Oxford University Press, 1998).

11. Kennell Jackson, *America Is Me: The Most Asked and Least Understood Questions about Black American History* (New York: Harper Collins, 1996), 109.

12. Brenda Stevenson, *Productions of Mrs. Maria W. Stewart* (Boston: W. Lloyd Garrison and Knapp, 1832); Jim Bearden and Linda Jean Butler, *Shadd: The Life and Times of Mary Ann Shadd* (Toronto: NC Press, 1977).

important way, Wilson inaugurated the African American literary tradition in a fundamentally *formal* manner."[13]

But it was Frances Ellen Watkins Harper who sustained the tradition of Black women in literature well into the late nineteenth century. Her poetry, short stories, and novels were popular "bestsellers" in the Black community, selling in the tens of thousands. And she was followed by a blossoming of writers, from Pauline Hopkins to Zora Neale Hurston to Gwendolyn Brooks and the extraordinary Black women of our own day.

The *creative voice* of Black women, which for our purposes includes all forms of creative activity other than music and writing, has found expression in everything from the sweet-grass baskets of South Carolina to the quilts of Harriet Powers (who lived from 1837 to 1911), to the sophisticated productions of Elizabeth Catlett and Artis Lane. Against a continuous background of folk art, such Black women as Edmonia Lewis (who was born in 1843, but we do not know when she died), the first known Black sculptor, have stepped into the artistic mainstream to "utter" in this especially effective voice.

For Black women the *adornment voice* has particular significance. Material considerations have often severely restricted the opportunities and resources for adornment, and the physical image of Black women has been made problematic by racialist mythology. Still, Black women have consistently expressed themselves through the decoration of their persons. In New Orleans in the 1800s, for example, a Roman Catholic city where women were required to wear head coverings on most occasions, Black women were forbidden to wear hats. The law was a clear attempt to favor white women and to prevent Black women from rivaling them in beauty adornment. The response of Black women was to develop elaborate headdresses from bright and beautifully printed fabric, which only enhanced their beauty. Later, in the late nineteenth and early twentieth centuries, Black woman entrepreneurs made fortunes in Black hair and beauty marketing.

In the post–Civil War emancipation, Reconstruction, and Jim

---

13. Harriet E. Wilson, *Our Nig*, ed. Henry Louis Gates Jr. (New York: Vintage Books, 1983).

Crow eras, newspaperwoman Ida B. Wells and writer Anna Julia Cooper formalized the voice—written and oral—of Black women publicly, but widespread lynching, rape, and disfranchisement forced the vast majority of their sisters into strategic silence and dissemblance. It is important to underscore that Black women's *dynamic voice* is evidenced through their resistance and protest, deeds and service, even when they did not write or speak in public. At every stage in the evolution of their voice, Black women have had to challenge conventional definitions of the proper place of women and of Black people in American society. Silent Black women constructed and privately affirmed positive identities and pursued their oppositional work out of the hearing and sight of dominant white power by creating special Black women's spaces of clubs and churches. They formulated methods of survival and of resistance while doing domestic work in white homes. Because they were not allowed to do their work in established institutions, Black women physicians built hospitals, teachers built schools, and other professionals formed alternative professional organizations, all expressions of the dynamic voice of Black women.

As we continue the process of evolving a sophisticated Black women's history, I implore us to attend to the following matters.

First, we must relentlessly seek to unveil the soul and probe the internal realities of Black women's lives and their relational networks that we and they have hidden and obscured.

Second, we must continue to pressure the institutions of our professions to recognize and accord legitimacy to Black women's history as a vital subfield within American history. Simultaneously, we must disseminate our scholarship and insights to broader, nonacademic audiences. We must situate Black women more concretely in southern women's history without erasure, and rewrite all of African American history to remove its masculinist bias and end the silencing of Black women through inattention to the issues and questions that concern them. This necessarily demands that we incorporate, wherever possible, the myriad voices of Black women to ensure that they remain collaborators in the histories that we write and teach.

Our greatest challenge as historians, however, is to recognize the limitations and shifting propensities of traditional power constructs and endeavor continuously to refine our frame of analysis.

Now, because I desire to end this presentation on a positive note, I say to all of my fellow historians of Black and white women of the South, let us proclaim to the world in one voice that we are doing good work and aim to keep at it until the job is done. And that is nothing less than the revisioning of American history.

About the Contributors

CAROL BLESER is the Kathryn and Calhoun Lemon Distinguished Professor of History at Clemson University and is currently President of the Southern Historical Association and past President of the Southern Association for Women Historians. A specialist in southern history, Professor Bleser has published *Tokens of Affection: The Letters of a Planter's Daughter in the Old South; In Joy and in Sorrow: Women, Family, and Marriage in the Victorian South; Secret and Sacred: The Diaries of James Henry Hammond, a Southern Slaveholder; The Hammonds of Redcliffe;* and *The Promised Land: The History of the South Carolina Land Commission, 1869-1890.* Professor Bleser is presently working on a book-length study of marriages in the mid-nineteenth-century South.

CATHERINE CLINTON is the Jones Distinguished Visiting Professor of History at Wofford College in Spartanburg, South Carolina. She is the author of several books, including *The Plantation Mistress, Tara Revisited,* and *Civil War Stories.* She is coeditor (with Nina Silber) of *Divided Houses: Gender and the Civil War* and (with Michele Gillespie) of *The Devil's Lane: Sex and Race in the Early South.*

MARY FREDERICKSON is an associate professor in history at Miami University of Ohio. She received her Ph.D. from the University of North Carolina at Chapel Hill in 1981, held a post-doctorate fellowship at the Wellesley College Center for Research on Women, and then joined the faculty at the University of Alabama in Birmingham until 1988. She is the author of many articles in women's history and labor history, and editor (with Joyce L. Kornbluh) of *Sisterhood and Solidarity: Women's Worker Education, 1914–1984.*

MICHELE GILLESPIE is Associate Professor of History at Agnes Scott College in Atlanta, Georgia. She is the coeditor of *The Devil's Lane: Sex and Race in the Early South* and the author of *Free Labor in an Unfree World: White Artisans in Slaveholding Georgia, 1789–1860.*

GLENDA ELIZABETH GILMORE is a native North Carolinian and Assistant Professor of History at Yale University. She graduated from Wake Forest University and earned an M.A. at the University of North Carolina at Charlotte. She received her Ph.D. from the University of North Carolina at Chapel Hill in 1992. Her book, *Gender and Jim Crow: Women and the Politics of White Supremacy in North Carolina, 1896–1920,* won the Frederick Jackson Turner Prize, the James A. Rawley Award, and the Julia Cherry Spruill Publication Prize.

DARLENE CLARK HINE is John A. Hannah Professor of American History at Michigan State University. Her most recent book, *A Shining Thread of Hope: The History of Black Women in America,* was coauthored by Kathleen Thompson. Her earlier books include *Speak Truth to Power: Black Professional Class in United States History, Hine Sight: Black Women and the Re-Construction of American History, Black Women in White: Racial Conflict and Cooperation in the Nursing Profession, 1890–1950,* and *Black Victory: The Rise and Fall of the White Primary in Texas.* She is editor of *The State of Afro-American History, Past, Present, and Future* and coeditor of a two-volume set, *Black Women in America: An Historical Encyclopedia.*

SUZANNE LEBSOCK, Professor of History at the University of Washington, is the author of *The Free Women of Petersburg*, which won the Bancroft Prize and the Berkshire Conference Book Prize in 1985, and *"A Share of Honour": Virginia Women, 1600-1945*. Formerly a member of the faculties of Rutgers University and the University of North Carolina at Chapel Hill, Lebsock moved to Seattle when her husband, Dick McCormick, became President of the University of Washington. They have two children, Betsy, thirteen, and Michael, nine.

JEAN B. LEE holds a Ph.D. in history from the University of Virginia and is on the faculty of the University of Wisconsin, Madison. The author of *The Price of Nationhood: The American Revolution in Charles County*, she has published widely on Chesapeake and Revolutionary history and is writing a book on Mount Vernon plantation during the period 1760–1865. Her current research explores how the memory and meaning of the Revolution were shaped in the century after Independence. While living in the South, Lee taught at the University of Alabama and the College of William and Mary and served as Director of the Institute of Early American History and Culture.

THEDA PERDUE is Professor of History at the University of North Carolina at Chapel Hill. She is author of *Slavery and the Evolution of Cherokee Society, 1540–1866, Native Carolinians*, and *The Cherokee*; editor of *Nations Remembered* and *Cherokee Editor*; coeditor of *Southern Women: Histories and Identities, Hidden Histories of Women in the New South*, and *The Cherokee Removal*. Her most recent work is *Cherokee Women: Gender and Culture Change*.

ANNE FIROR SCOTT, W. K. Boyd Professor of History Emerita at Duke University, was a pioneer in the second phase of southern women's history and was President of the Organization of American Historians and the Southern Historical Association. In *Unheard Voices* she traced the history of her predecessors: the first historians of southern women.

VIRGINIA VAN DER VEER HAMILTON received her A.B. and M.A. degrees from Birmingham-Southern College. After a twenty-year career in journalism in Washington, D.C., and Alabama, she became the second woman to receive a Ph.D. in history from the University of Alabama, Tuscaloosa. She taught at Alabama College (now the University of Montevallo) and Birmingham-Southern before affiliating with the University of Alabama at Birmingham, where she chaired the History Department for eight years. She is the author of seven books, including biographies of Supreme Court Justice Hugo Black and U.S. Senator Lister Hill, the Bicentennial history of Alabama, and national prize–winning public school textbooks on Alabama history. Her articles and essays, written for the Associated Press, the *New York Times, American Heritage*, the *International Herald-Tribune*, and other journals, along with reflections on her pioneering career as a journalist and historian, appear in her most recent book, *Looking for Clark Gable and Other Twentieth-Century Pursuits: Collected Writings*. She is an elected Fellow of the Society of American Historians. She was married for forty-five years until her husband's death; their daughter, Carol, teaches English at Carnegie-Mellon University; their son, David, is in hotel management.

Index

Abby, Kathryn Trimmer, 9, 147, 150–52, 156
Abernathy, T. P., 69
Abolitionists. *See* Antislavery
Abortion, 20
Adair, James, 87, 91, 93
Adams, Charles Francis, 98
Adams, John, 105
Adultery, 88
Agriculture, 16, 17, 18
Alabama, University of: at Birmingham, 6, 73; at Huntsville, 75, 76, 78
Alabama College for Women, 71, 72, 73, 79
Alden, John Richard, 69
Alexander, Thomas B., 74
American Association of University Professors (AAUP), 148, 149
American Association of University Women (AAUW), 148, 149
American Historical Association (AHA), 65, 116, 150
American Mill (Bessemer City, N.C.), 24, 25
American Political Science Association (APSA), 65
American Revolution: daily experiences, 7; significance, 97; public awareness of, 97, 100; current historiography, 103–10; tyranny, 104; rural communities, 104; place, 104–5; women's contributions, 108; communal cooperation, 108–9; effects of war, 109–10; mentioned, 96, 113

American Woman Suffrage Association (AWSA), 81
Anderson, Fred, 107
Antebellum America, 43, 45, 53
Anthony, Susan B., 115
Anthony Amendment, 35, 36
Antislavery, 48, 50–51, 52–53, 59, 61
Antisuffragists: on universal suffrage, 6; compared with suffragists, 30; legislators, 35; behavior, 36; exploit race arguments, 38, 41; mentioned, 30, 33
Asante, Kariamu Welshe, 169
Asheville, N.C., 22
Athens, Ga., 21
Athens College, 78, 79

Bailyn, Bernard, 102
Bancroft, George, 114
Barrett, Bernice, 163
Barth, Alan, 69
Beale, Howard, 154
Beard, Charles, 65
Beard, Mary Ritter, 65–66, 67, 80, 117
Beman, Nathan: Mount Zion Academy, 146
Berkeley, Kathleen, 163
Bessemer City, N.C., 24, 25, 26
Bigotry, 31, 41
Billington, Monroe Lee, 69
Birth control, 20
Birthrate, 20
Black newspapers, 38, 41, 131
Black women: protest history, 4; beyond traditional, 10; autobiography,

179

Black women (*cont.*)
10, 159–60, 165, 166; March on
Washington, 23; as workers, 15,
16, 18, 23, 25; suffrage, 33, 164;
transformative, 164; registering, 37;
toward democracy, 42; political activism, 136; focus on social history,
159; framework, 159, 167; trends,
160–73; literature, 161–63; need for
separate history, 163–64; further investigation, 165; soul, 166; connection with white women, 167, 168;
challenge to historians, 167,
172–73; goal, 168; strategies,
168–69; forms of voice, 169–72; oppositional work, 172
Bleser, Carol, 9, 11
"Bloody Kansas," 47
Boatwright, Eleanor, 118
Bossu, Jean-Bernard, 90
Bourbon County, Ky., 97
Bourdieu, Pierre, 128, 139, 144
Bowen, Catherine Drinker, 67, 68, 80
Brandon, Betty, 4
Brittain, Elizabeth, 22
Brooks, Gwendolyn, 171
Brooks, Preston, 54, 56
Brown, Elsa Barkley, 136, 139, 161,
162, 164
Brown, John: gendered sectionalism,
6; Harpers Ferry, 6, 59; image, 56;
reactions to Sack of Lawrence, 56,
59; raid, 56–59; link with Sumner,
56, 61–62; debut, 57; on Fugitive
Slave Law, 57; political repercus-
sions, 59–60; sexual language, 60;
symbol, 60–61; legacy, 61, 63
Brown, Kathleen, 11
Brown, University of, 72
Brown's Station: Osawatomie, 57;
mentioned, 58
Bruce, Kathleen, 151
Bryan, Maria, 145, 146, 147
Bryson City, N.C., 24
Bull, Jonathan, 46
Bull, Mary, 46, 48
Burns, James McGregor, 69
Burr, Virginia Ingraham, 154
Butler, Andrew, 52, 54
Bynum, Victoria, 136
Byrd, William, 92

Callicutt, Elizabeth, 18
Carby, Hazel, 164
Carter, Dan, 128
Cary, Mary Ann Shadd, 170
Cary, N.C., 19
Cash, W. J.: "Mind of the South," 127;
southern men, 137
Catlett, Elizabeth, 171
Catt, Carrie Chapman, 36–37
Chapman, Maria Weston, 50–51
Charles County, Md., 105, 107–8, 109
Charleston, S.C., 156
Charlotte, N.C., 137
Cherokee, N.C., 24
Cherokees: Booger Dance, 92; Trail
of Tears, 142; mentioned, 86, 87,
91, 94
Chesapeake, 106, 107
Chesnut, Mary Boykin, 80, 155
Chicago, Ill., 36
Chicago, University of, 117
Chickasaw Nation, 93, 94
Child, L. Maria, 50–51, 61, 112
Choctaws, 93, 94
Civil Rights Movement, 127
Civil War, 97, 99, 100, 115
Clark, Adele, 32, 40
Clark-Lewis, Elizabeth, 162
Claude, Mildred, 74, 78, 79
Clemson University, 9, 157
Clinton, Catherine, 6, 11, 163
Colden, Cadwallader, 89
Cold War, 127–28
Collective action, 4, 18, 22–23. *See also*
Women workers
College of Charleston, 3
Columbian Exposition, 114, 115
Columbus, Christopher, 7, 82, 83,
93–93, 95
Columbus, N.C., 22
Commager, Henry Steele, 67
Congress, 36, 48, 53, 106, 108
Connecticut Anti-Slavery, 51
Constitution: of U.S., 30; of Virginia,
34; mentioned, 34, 100
Continental Army, 97, 101, 107, 108
Copeland, Issac, 154
Cook, Marjorie Howell, 74
Cooper, Anna Julia, 172
Cornell University, 71
Cott, Nancy, 65, 66

Cotton, Everlina Jane, 19, 20
Cox, Isaac J., 151
Cox, LaWanda, 156
Craven, Avery, 150
Creeks, 89, 94
Crocker, Hannah Mather, 112
Croly, Jane, 115–16

Dailey, Jane, 139
Darwin, Charles, 120
Declaration of Independence, 97, 98, 100
De Cuneo, Michele, 83, 84
Deerfield, Mass., 169
Delany, Elizabeth, 96
Delany, Sarah, 96
Democrats, 31, 39, 133, 134
Dennett, Tyler, 150
DePauw University, 65
Der Veer Hamilton, Virginia Van, 4, 6, 11
Divorce, 22
Dodd, Dorothy, 151
Donald, David, 55, 154
Doss, Harriet Amos, 77
Doster, James E., 73
Douglas, Ann, 50
Douglass, Frederick, 61
Doyle, John, 58
Doyle, Mahala, 58
Dred Scott decision (1857), 48
Dubois, W. E. B., 56, 57, 61–62, 140–41
Duke University, 8, 71, 156
Dunham, Katherine, 169

East, Charles, 80
Edwards, Laura, 136, 143
Ellett, Elizabeth, 113
Emerson, Ralph Waldo, 62
Engels, Friedrich, 143
Equal Rights Amendment, 2
Equal Suffrage League, 31, 33, 34, 41

Family planning, 20
Farmer, Dr. Hallie, 71, 72, 80
Farnham, Christie, 163
Feeling, Nicholas, 70
Feminism, 37–38, 41, 114, 119; and prefeminist condition, 124
Fielding, Sarah, 115
Fields, Barbara, 40–41

Fifteenth Amendment, 36
Finkelman, Paul, 61
Florida State College for Woman, 150
Florida State University, 150
Foner, Eric, 81
Forbes, Esther, 67, 68, 80
Foucault, Michel, 143
Fox-Genovese, Elizabeth, 135–36, 163
Franklin, John Hope, 154
Frederickson, Mary, 5, 10–11
Free-Soil Party, 53
Fugitive Slave Law, 57
Fuller, Margaret: "Conversations," 114

Garraty, John, 81
Gaston, Paul, 69
Gaston County, N.C., 25, 27
Gastonia, N.C., 24
Gates, Henry Louis, Jr., 164, 170
Gearhart, Va., 118
Geary, Patrick, 80
Gender: shaper, 9; in South, 48; women's rights movement, 52; prejudice, 64; southern politics, 125, 128–29; connected to race, 130; solidarity limitations, 135; perceptions of southern historians, 137; male constructs, 137–38; Engels, 143; as a frame, 167; mentioned, 45, 126, 127
Giddings, Paula, 162
Gilead: John Brown's utopia, 57
Gilmore, Glenda, 9, 163
Glymph, Thavolia, 163
Grantham, Dewey, 154
Greene, Nathaniel, 99
Green, Fletcher, 154
Green, Ollie Foster, 22
Griffith, Dr. Lucille, 71, 72, 76, 79
Grimké, Angelina, 47, 60
Grimké, Sarah, 47, 60, 112–13
Goodrich, Samuel, 113
Gordon, Kate, 41
Goucher College, 118, 147

Hale, Sarah Josepha, 113
Halkerston, Ann, 106
Hall, Gwendolyn, 11
Hall, Jacquelyn, 136, 144
Hammond, James Henry, 54

Harley, Sharon, 161
Harper, Frances Ellen Watkins, 170, 171
Harpers Ferry. *See* Brown, John
Harvard University, 117
Hawthorne, Nathaniel, 46, 47
Hayden, Ala., 21
Heath, Frederick, 156
Hendricks, Wanda, 163, 164
Hendrix College, 152
Henry, Patrick, 32
Higginbotham, Evelyn Brooks, 161, 162, 164
Hill, Mary Wright, 22
Hine, Darlene Clark, 10, 165
Hodes, Martha, 136, 149
Hollins College, 151
Honor, 48, 55, 62, 137
Hood College, 150
Hopkins, Pauline, 171
Houston, Nora, 40
Hull, Gloria, 164
Hunter, Tera, 162
Huntersville, N.C., 18, 19
Hurston, Zora Neale, 171

Illiteracy, 34
Incest, 88, 91
International Federation of University Women (IFUW): Norway 1924, 148
Interracial coalitions, 23
Interracial movement, 40
Iowa University, 71

Jackson, Andrew, 142
Jacobs, Harriet, 165, 170
Jameson, J. Franklin, 150
Jamestown, Virginia, 83, 84
Jamison, Judith, 169
Janiewski, Dolores, 163
Jefferson, Thomas: on suffrage, 32; on Native American customs, 85, 86; Declaration of Independence, 97; mentioned, 98, 103, 106
Jim Crow, 36, 134, 141, 171–72
Johns Hopkins University, 116
Johnson, Daisy, 21–22
Johnson, Guion Griffis, 118
Johnson, Sarah, 28, 29
Johnston, Mary, 34, 41
Jones, Catherine, 18

Jones, Jacqueline, 163
Joyner, Charles, 104
Judson College, 79

Kansas-Nebraska Act of 1854, 53
Kansas Volunteers, 58
Kantrowitz, Steven, 138
Keckley, Elizabeth, 45
Keeney, Barney, 72, 73
Kelley, Abby, 50–51
Kelly, Robin D. G., 139
Kentucky, University of, 9–10
Kerber, Linda, 49
King, Wilma, 162, 165
Kingsland, Alma, 19
Knoxville, Tenn., 36
Kraditor, Aileen, 29–30, 32, 41
Ku Klux Klan, 127

Labor activism, 22, 27
Larkin, Margaret, 26
Lawson, John, 87, 89, 90
League of Women Voters, 118, 121
Lebsock, Suzanne, 5, 11
Lee, Jean, 7, 11
Lee, Robert E., 32
Lenox Hall, Saint Louis, 150
Lerner, Gerda, 161
Lewis, Edmonia, 171
Liberty Guard, 58
Lincoln, Abraham, 98, 100
Lindbergh, Anne, 65
Lindbergh, Charles, 65
Literacy test, 34, 37
Littlefield, Valinda, 163
Livermore, Mary, 11
Longe, Alexander, 89
Lonn, Ella, 9, 147–48, 149, 156
Loray Mill (Gastonia, N.C.), 25
Louisville, Ky., 2
Lovejoy, Elijah, 60
Luck, Madame, 19
Lumpkin, Katharine Du Pre, 127, 141

McCurry, Stephanie, 11, 138, 143
McDowell, Deborah, 164
McKay, Claude: "Baptism," 158
McLaurin, Melton, 80
Madison, James, 45–46, 97, 98, 99
Maier, Pauline, 102
Manly, Alexander, 131, 142

Manville-Jenckes Company, 25, 26
March on Washington (1963), 23
Marshall, John, 32
Maryland, 97
Masculine, 43, 48
Masculinity, 52, 137
Mason, George, 32
Mason, Lucy Randolph, 32
Massachusetts, 104
Massey, Mary Elizabeth, 9, 147, 152–54, 155, 156
Mendenhall, Margery, 118
Miami University, 5
Michigan State University, 10
Miles, Edwin, 154
Missouri: Compromise, 45; mentioned, 48, 57
Mitchell, Margaret, 80
Montevallo, University of. *See* Alabama College for Women
Montgomery, Ala., 23
Morgan County, Ga., 19
Morrilton, Ark., 152
Morse, Jedidiah, 88
Mossell, Gertrude, 116
Mott, Lucretia, 50
Mount Vernon, 100
Mount Zion Academy, 146
Mount Zion, Ga., 145
Murray, Judith Sergeant, 112, 119–20

Naire, Thomas, 89
National American Woman Suffrage Association (NAWSA), 37
National Association of Colored Women's Clubs (NACWC), 127
National Textile Workers Union (NTWU), 25, 26
Native Americans: and sex, 4, 7, 85, 86, 87–88, 90–91; women, 83, 84; and Europeans, 83, 84, 86, 92; clothing, 85; Thomas Jefferson and, 85, 86; tattoos, 85–86; courtship, 86; incest, 88, 91; polygyny, 88; marriage, 89; matrilineal, 89; paternity, 89; violence against women, 92; rape during war, 93; land ownership, 94
Negrotown, N.C., 20
Neverdon-Morton, Cynthia, 161, 162
Nevins, Allan, 154

New Deal, 127
New Haven, Conn., 51
Newport News, Va., 37
Nichols, Roy F., 150
Nineteenth Amendment, 35, 38, 134
Norfolk, Va., 28
Norfolk Equal Suffrage League, 32
Northwestern University, 150

Old South, 44
Oral history, 113
Organization of American Historians (OAH), 2, 8
Osawatomie, Kans.: John Brown, 57
Ownby, Ted, 137
Owsley, Frank, 73

Painter, Nell, 139, 154, 162
Parkman, Francis, 114
Parks, Rosa, 23
Patriarchy, 44, 131
Patrick, Rembert, 154
Patriotism, 98, 100
Peabody University, 71
Peery, Janet, 102
Penarchy, 44–45
Pennsylvania, University of, 75, 77
Perdue, Theda, 7, 11
Peterson, Cornelia, 19
Peterson, Paul, 124
Phallocracy, 44
Philadelphia, Pa., 50
Philippe, Louis, 86, 92
Phillips, Ulrich Bonnell, 69, 125, 126, 129
Phillips, William, 57
Pitcher, Molly, 101
Plantations, 44, 45, 48
Pocahontas, 7, 82, 85, 95
Political history, 9, 30–31, 124–25, 128–29, 136
Populist Party: southern politics, 126; interracial coalition, 131; split with Democrats, 133; racial ideology, 134
Port Tobacco, Md., 105
Potawatomie Rifles, 58
Potomac River, 105
Powers, Harriet, 171
Powhatans, 83
Prescott, William, 114

Prince, Lucy Terry, 169, 170
Princeton University, 117
Progressive Movement, 135
Proslavery, 48, 50, 57
Prostitution, 87–88
Prynne, Hester, 47
Pyron, Darden Asbury, 80

Race: shaper, 9; Native Americans, 92; in southern politics, 125, 128–29; and gender, 130; as a frame, 167; mentioned, 126, 127, 141, 160
Race baiting, 31, 41
Racism: to advance suffrage, 41, 164; mentioned, 40, 143
Raleigh, N.C., 19, 20
Ramsay, John, 73, 74
Ransby, Barbara, 162
Ratcliffe, Governor, 95
Reconstruction, 126, 139, 144, 171
Redpath, James, 61
Reed, Linda, 165
Reform Movements, 32
Republican Party, 31, 42, 53, 126, 131
Richmond, University of, 6
Richmond, Va., 37, 39
Richmond Suffrage League, 32
Roberts, Frances, 73, 74, 75, 76, 78, 79
Roberts vs. Boston: and Sumner, 53
Rochester, University of, 72
Rock Hill, S.C., 152
Rollins College, 151
Romans, Bernard, 87
Roosevelt, Eleanor, 65
Roosevelt, Franklin, 65
Rose, Willie Lee, 3
Rouse, Jacquelyn, 11, 162
Ruffin, Virginia Edmund, 62
Rush, Benjamin, 85–86, 96
Russell, Mattie, 154

Sage, Mrs. Russell, 116
Salary, 77–79, 148, 149. See also Wages
Savannah, Ga., 21
Schama, Simon, 70, 80
Schlesinger Library. See Woman's Archives at Radcliffe
Schwalm, Leslie, 163
Scott, Anne, 8, 11, 135, 156
Scottsboro trials, 73

Sectional conflict, 6, 43, 44, 45, 50, 56
Seed, Patricia, 11
Segregation, 31, 141
Seminoles, 94
Sex: harassment, 2; objectification of, 7; equality, 10; biracial slaves, 44; physical restraints, 45; identity and penarchy, 45; dynamic in colonization, 82, 84; as a commodity, 88; abuse by Native Americans, 92; misbehavior of Europeans, 92
Sexuality: interpretations of past, 43; women's rights movement, 52; flaunted, 85; Native American lack of clothing, 85; interracial, 131; Foucault, 143; as a frame, 167
Sexual license, 48
Sexual politics, 44, 47, 60
Sexual violence, 93, 95
Shalhope, Robert E., 70, 102
Shannon, Frederick A., 150
Shaw, Stephanie, 162
Shepard, Wynss, 75, 77
Sherman, William, 58
Simon, Bryant, 138
Simpson, Craig, 62
Simpson, Phoebe, 22
Sims, Anastatia, 11
Slaves: black women, 15; and owners, 44, 45, 53; in Hawthorne, 47; Grimké sisters' views, 47; antislave image, 52–53; insurrection among, 61; in colonial period, 103; and plantations, 146
Smith, David C., 80
Smith, John, 82–83, 95
Smith, Susan, 163
Smoot, Elmira, 21
Solidarity: and gender, 135
Sororal polygyny, 88, 91
Southern Association for Women Historians (SAWH): established, 2; founders' goals, 2; conferences, 3, 4, 9; list of presidents, 13; anniversary, 147; mentioned, 12, 81, 156
Southern character, 49. See also Honor
Southern Historical Association (SHA): and SAWH, 2, 4; Anne Scott, 8; women presidents, 9, 147, 148, 156; growth of women's movement, 154–55; mentioned, 154

Southern historiography, 125–27
Southern history, 134–40
Southern Industrial Revolution, 17
Southern women: white gloves, 1, 5; education's role, 5; stereotypes, 15; black women, 15; significant groups, 16; and economy, 16; courtship, 19; marriage, 19; childbearing and prevention, 20; collective protest, 22–23; reaction to Sumner, 55
Southern Women for the Prevention of Lynching, 81
Southern women workers, 16–17, 18, 20–21, 22, 23, 27
Spaniards: "black legend," 83
Spruill, Julia Cherry, 2–3, 118
Stanford University, 71
Stanton, Elizabeth Cady, 51–52, 115
Status of Women in College and University Faculties, 149
Stevenson, Brenda, 162
Stewart, Jeffrey, 80
Stewart, Maria, 170
Stowe, Steven, 137
Strachey, William, 85
Strikes, 25, 26
Strong, George Templeton, 55
Suffrage: A. Elizabeth Taylor, 3; in Virginia, 5, 28, 31, 33, 34, 42; debates, 29, 35, 38, 115; in Aileen Kraditor, 29–30; state level, 30; racial arguments, 31, 41, 164; propaganda, 32; black women, 33, 164; response to opposition, 33–34; amendment, 33, 34, 35; black political supremacy, 36; in black newspapers, 38; for white women only, 127; mentioned, 32, 40, 114, 121
Suffrage Movement, 30, 35, 66, 117–18
Suffragists, 29, 30, 33, 37, 38, 40, 164
Sumner, Charles, 53, 54, 55, 56, 61–62
Sumner-Brooks 1856, 53
Taylor, A. Elizabeth, 3, 154
Terborg-Penn, Rosalyn, 161, 162, 164
Texas, University of, 72
Textile industry, 23
Thomas, Ella Gertrude Clanton, 153, 154
Thompson, Kathleen, 166

Tindall, George, 69, 154
Tobacco industry, 23
Troy Female Seminary, 114, 116
Truth, Sojourner, 170
Tubman, Harriet, 57
Tuchman, Barbara, 67, 80
Tyron, N.C., 18

Unions, 23, 25
United States League of Gileadites. See Brown, John

Valentine, Lila Meade, 34, 41
Vanderbilt University, 72, 73
Veer Hamilton, Virginia Van der. See Der Veer Hamilton, Virginia Van
Vespucci, Amerigo, 85
Violence: against working women, 22; sexual power, 45; defending honor, 48, 56; beating, 141; lynching, 172; rape, 172
Virginia, 34, 37–38, 41, 92
Virginia, University of, 38
Virginia Association Opposed to Woman Suffrage, 33
Virginia Constitution 1902, 31, 40
Voluntary Associations, 114
Voter registration, 39

Wages, 16, 17, 21, 22. See also Salary
Wake County, N.C., 19
Walker, Maggie, 39
Wallace, Alfred Russell, 120
Walter, Ronald, 52
Washington, D.C., 36
Washington, George, 101
Washington, Martha, 101
Washington, Mary Helen, 164
Washington, University of, 5
Weaver, Blanche Clark, 156
Webster, Daniel, 100
Wells, Ida B., 172
Wheatley, Phillis, 170
Wheeler, Marjorie Spruill, 11
White, Deborah Gray, 162
White supremacy: gendered, 5, 138; suffrage debates, 29; suffragists' feelings, 29, 34; securing, 31; argument, 33; opposition, 36; endangered, 37; as southern distinctiveness, 125; moves to

White supremacy (*cont.*)
eradicate, 127; gender and race, 127; after civil rights, 128; center, 131; depiction of white women, 133; naturalize racial oppression, 139; understanding, 144; mentioned, 30, 32, 40, 41, 132, 143
Wiggins, Ella May, 23–27
Wiley, Bell, 154
Wiley, Evelyn, 77, 79
Wilkinson, Allen, 58
Willard, Emma, 114
Willard, Frances, 116
Williams, Harry T., 154
Williams, Selina, 19, 21
Wilmington racial massacre, 130–31
Wilson, Edmund, 67
Wilson, Harriet, 170
Wilson, Mattie J., 19
Winthrop College, 152
Wisconsin, University of, 7, 71, 117, 118
Wise, Henry, 62
Wollstonecraft, Mary, 112
Woman's Archives at Radcliffe, 66, 117. *See also* Beard, Mary Ritter
Women historians: sex discrimination, 6; equality, 6–7; activism, 8; status of, 10, 156–57; history in profession, 11; label, 64; nonprofessional categories, 68–70; prior to WWII, 71; post WWII, 72–76; camaraderie with males, 75–76; as department heads, 76; salaries, 77–79; challenges, 81, 157; suggestions, 149; problems, 155
Women workers: collective action, 4, 18, 23; importance of, 5, 17, 27; effect of stereotype, 15; mills, 16; agriculture, 16, 17; prior to WWII, 17; young girls, 18; black women, 18, 23; and Wiggins's story, 27
Women's associations, 115
Women's Christian Temperance Union (WCTU), 81, 117, 131
Women's history: importance of writings, 9, 115; future, 11–12; woman as a label, 44; property holding, 106; spinsters/widows, 106; changing, 111; and women's activism, 112, 117, 120; voluntary associations, 114; nascent consciousness, 114; growth, 119
Women's Rights Movement, 30, 48, 52, 66, 114
Woodward, C. Vann: self-referential writing, 140; mentioned, 68, 77, 80, 125, 128, 129
Woolf, Virginia, 115
World War I, 16, 18
World War II, 17, 118, 127
Wyatt-Brown, Bertram, 49, 137

Yale University, 71, 117
Yellin, Jean, 47
Yorktown, Battle of, 105

Acknowledgments

Glenda Elizabeth Gilmore's essay is to be published in *Feminist Studies* (spring 1999) and is used here with permission.

Suzanne Lebsock's essay first appeared in *Visible Women: New Essays on American Activism*, ed. Nancy Hewitt and Suzanne Lebsock (1993) and is used here with the permission of the University of Illinois Press.

Theda Perdue's essay appeared originally in *Southern Cultures*, published by the University of North Carolina Press for the University of North Carolina Center for the Study of the American South, and is used with permission.

Anne Firor Scott's essay appeared originally in *Journal of Women's History* and is used here with the permission of Indiana University Press.

Virginia Van der Veer Hamilton's essay is adapted from a selection that first appeared in *Looking for Clark Gable and Other Twentieth-Century Pursuits: Collected Writings* (1996) and is used here with the permission of the University of Alabama Press.